STARTER

STUDENT'S BOOK AND WORKBOOK

with Digital Pack

COMBO B

CEFR A1

AMERICAN TH!NK

SECOND EDITION

Herbert Puchta,
Jeff Stranks &
Peter Lewis-Jones

CAMBRIDGE UNIVERSITY PRESS

CONTENTS

Vowel sound /ɔr/	**Values:** The importance of sports	**Reading** Article: Sports wonders! Article: An amazing last four minutes **Writing** Paragraph: My favorite athlete **Listening** Phone call: Making arrangements
Intonation – listing items	**Values:** Music **Train to THINK:** Memorizing	**Reading** Microblogs: #Musicintheforest Dialogue: An interview with a teenage DJ **Writing** Microblogs: Describing a scene **Listening** Radio program: Musicians around the world

TOWARDS A2 Key for Schools practice

Intonation – giving two choices	**Values:** How you eat is important	**Reading** Article: Kitchen kids Menu and dialogue: In a restaurant **Writing** Menu: A meal plan for your friend **Listening** Dialogue: Cooking
Simple past regular verbs	**Values:** Hard work and achievement **Train to THINK:** Sequencing	**Reading** Article: She was the first woman in space Article: Sports achievers **Writing** Proposal: A statue in my town **Listening** Dialogue: An awards ceremony at school

TOWARDS A2 Key for Schools practice

Simple past irregular verbs	**Values:** Animals and us	**Reading** Article: Dolphins to the rescue Article: Extinct animals **Writing** Short text: An extinct animal **Listening** Dialogue: Josh's vacation
Word stress – comparatives	**Values:** Transportation and the environment **Train to THINK:** Comparing	**Reading** Article: The great race Article: My favorite trip **Writing** Description: Unusual forms of transportation **Listening** Dialogue: At the train station

TOWARDS A2 Key for Schools practice

Pronunciation pages 121–122

Get it right! pages 125–126

Speaking activities pages 127–128

7 LIVING FOR SPORTS

OBJECTIVES

FUNCTIONS: talking about abilities; telling the time; talking about routines and dates; making suggestions

GRAMMAR: *can* (ability); prepositions of time

VOCABULARY: sports; telling the time; months and seasons; ordinal numbers

Get THINKING

Watch the video and think: What are your favorite sports?

A ☐ ____________

C ☐ ____________

B ☐ ____________

D ☐ ____________

READING

1 **Match the sports in the list with the photos. Write 1–4 in the boxes.**

1 soccer | 2 rock climbing | 3 snowboarding | 4 surfing

2 **Look at Exercise 1. In which sports do you do these actions?**

1 kick
2 pull
3 stand
4 run
5 turn
6 swim

3 SPEAKING **Do you play any of the sports in the photos? Tell your partner.**

4 7.01 **Read and listen to the article. Write the names under the photos in Exercise 1.**

Goatee | Maureen | Nikolai | Sloan

5 **Read the article again. Check (✓) the correct box for each sentence.**

	True	False	Doesn't say
0 Nikolai only uses his feet and legs to stop the ball from falling.		✓	
1 Nikolai can do this for more than a day.			
2 Sloan is 14 years old.			
3 Sloan goes very fast on the snowboard.			
4 Maureen was born with no hands.			
5 Maureen doesn't think she is different from other climbers.			
6 Goatee is a young goat.			
7 Goatee can swim very well.			

SPORTS WONDERS!

Nikolai Kutsenko, from Ukraine, can do amazing things with a soccer ball. He can kick a ball well … but he can also keep the ball in the air with his feet, legs, and head. A lot of soccer players can do this. But can they do it for 24 hours and 30 minutes without stopping? Nikolai can and it's a world record!

Sloan Henderson, from Utah, is a really good snowboarder – and she's only 14 months old! Her mother and father take her to the mountains and they put her on a snowboard – and there she goes! Sloan loves to be on the board. People are often surprised when they see her because she doesn't fall down!

American rock climber **Maureen "Mo" Beck** was born without her left hand and only part of her left arm, but she can climb really well. She is the winner of two climbing World Championships for disabled athletes and five national championships. She has her own special way of climbing, but Maureen thinks she is just the same as any other climber.

Goatee can't talk or write, but she can surf! Why is this special? Because Goatee is a goat! She surfs with her owner, Dana McGregor. Dana helps Goatee to stand on the board and together they ride the waves in California. Goatee wears a yellow life jacket because she can't swim very well! And now there is a children's book about her, too – Dana is the author.

THINK values

The importance of sports

6 **Why do people play sports? Read the reasons below and add two more of your own. Put these reasons in order of importance. Write 1–8 in the boxes.**

- ☐ It's fun.
- ☐ You can make friends.
- ☐ It's good to win.
- ☐ ____________________
- ☐ ____________________
- ☐ It's easy.
- ☐ It's healthy.
- ☐ It's exciting.

7 SPEAKING **Work in pairs and compare your ideas.**

People play sports because it's fun.

GRAMMAR
can (ability)

1 **Look at the article on page 67 and complete the sentences. Then complete the rule and the table.**

1 He ___________ kick a ball well.
2 ___________ they do it for 24 hours?
3 She ___________ swim very well.

> **RULE:** We use [4]___________ to talk about ability.
> The negative form is [5]___________ .
> We don't use *do*/*does* with *can* in questions or negative forms.

Positive	Negative
I/you/we/he/she/it/they can jump.	I/you/we/he/she/it/they [6]___________ (**cannot**) jump.
Questions	**Short answers**
[7]___________ I/you/we/he/she/it/they jump?	Yes, I/you/we/he/she/it/they **can**. No, I/you/we/he/she/it/they **can't**.

2 **Write sentences about John with *can* or *can't*.**

0 swim ✓
John can swim.
1 sing ✗
2 cook ✓
3 play the piano ✗
4 dance ✗
5 ride a bike ✓

PRONUNCIATION
Long vowel sound /ɔː/ Go to page 121.

3 **Look at the activities in the list. Check (✓) the things you can do.**

- ☐ play tennis
- ☐ stand on your head
- ☐ throw a ball 20 meters
- ☐ spell your name in English
- ☐ count to 20 in English
- ☐ say the alphabet in under 10 seconds
- ☐ surf
- ☐ make a cake
- ☐ play the guitar
- ☐ jump really high

4 SPEAKING **Work in pairs. Ask and answer the questions from Exercise 3.**

Can you count to 20 in English?

Yes, I can. 1, 2, 3, 4, …

→ workbook page 64

VOCABULARY
Sports

5 7.04 **Match the words in the list with the photos. Write 1–8 in the boxes. Listen and check.**

1 cycle | **2** dive | **3** do gymnastics | **4** do Taekwondo | **5** play basketball | **6** play volleyball | **7** skateboard | **8** ski

A ☐

E ☐

B ☐

F ☐

C ☐

G ☐

D ☐

H ☐

6 SPEAKING **Work in pairs. Which of these sports can/can't you do? Tell your partner.**

I can ski, but I can't dive.

→ workbook page 66

VOCABULARY
Telling the time

7 7.05 **Match the times in the list with the clocks. Write 1–4 in the boxes. Listen and check.**

1 It's eight thirty. | 2 It's three o'clock.
3 It's a quarter after ten. | 4 It's a quarter to one.

A ☐ B ☐ C ☐ D ☐

8 SPEAKING **Work in pairs. Write the times under the clocks. Then ask and answer.**

What's the time?

It's a quarter after four.

0 *It's a quarter after four.*

2 ______________________

1 ______________________

3 ______________________

→ workbook page 66

LISTENING

9 7.06 **Listen to a phone call between Mike and Julia. When do they decide to go cycling?**

10 7.06 **Listen again. Check (✓) the sports you hear.**

- a tennis ☐
- b cycling ☐
- c basketball ☐
- d volleyball ☐
- e golf ☐
- f Taekwondo ☐

11 7.06 **Listen again. Match the clocks and the sentences. Write 1–8 in the boxes.**

1 The Taekwondo class starts at ...
2 The Taekwondo class finishes at ...
3 The tennis lesson is at ...
4 The tennis lesson finishes at ...
5 It gets dark at ...
6 The basketball game finishes at ...
7 The basketball game starts at ...
8 The time now is ...

12 **Think of four things you do every day. Draw the time that you do them on clocks in your notebook.**

13 SPEAKING **Work in pairs. Look at your partner's clocks. Guess what he/she does at each time. Use the things below or your own ideas.**

get up | have breakfast
start school | play sports
do your homework | do your homework
go to bed

Do you get up at six thirty?

Do you have breakfast at ...?

SPEAKING

14 **Look at the example of a time-cake then draw a time-cake for you.**

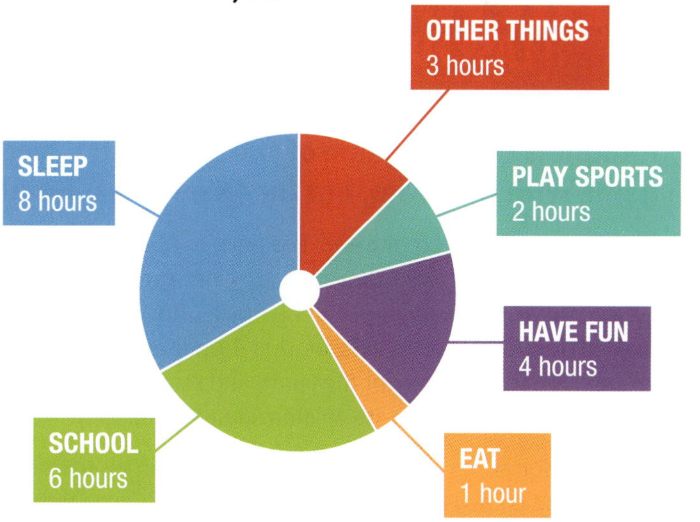

15 **Work in pairs. Talk about your time-cake.**

1 Are you happy with your time-cake?
2 Would you like to change it? How?

16 **Work in pairs. Draw your ideal time-cake. Compare with your partner.**

READING

1 SPEAKING **Work in pairs. Discuss these questions.**

1 What do you know about basketball? How long is a game? How do players score points?
2 What are the best basketball teams?

2 7.07 **Read and listen to the article. Why are the last four minutes amazing?**

3 **Read the first paragraph again. Mark the statements T (true) or F (false).**

1 Jason helps the players on the school team. ☐
2 Jason practices basketball three times a week. ☐
3 Jason plays on his high school basketball team. ☐
4 Jason plays in the first game of the season. ☐

4 **Read the last two paragraphs again. Put the events in order.**

a The coach tells him to go and play. ☐
b Jason scores a 3-point basket. ☐
c The crowd is really happy. ☐
d Jason watches from the bench. 1
e Jason scores six 3-pointers. ☐
f Jason misses a shot. ☐

5 SPEAKING **Work in pairs. Choose a sport you both like. Imagine an amazing ending to a game / competition. Tell others in the class about it.**

Do you like tennis?

Yes, it's my favorite sport. Let's imagine an amazing ending to a tennis game.

AN AMAZING LAST FOUR MINUTES

It's February 15th at Greece Athena High School, New York. Jason McElwain is an 18-year-old student. Jason is autistic. He loves basketball and he helps with the school basketball team. Jason practices hard every day, but he never plays on the team.

Tonight is the last game of the season. It's Jason's last chance to play a game with the team, but for 44 minutes, he sits on the bench and watches.

It's four minutes before the end. The team is winning, so the coach tells Jason to go out and play. The team and the crowd are very happy, because everyone knows Jason and likes him. Jason tries to score a basket, but he misses. But suddenly he gets a 3-point basket. The crowd goes crazy. Jason gets another 3-pointer, then another and another – he gets six 3-pointers (it's a record for the team) and scores twenty points altogether. The team wins and Jason is a real hero. It's an amazing night for him!

Soon Jason starts to become famous. People in his town know who he is. The US president comes to Jason's town to meet him. Jason writes a book and some people want to make a movie about him. He becomes assistant coach to the high school basketball team.

Now Jason works hard to help other autistic people. He travels across the US to help get money for autism research.

VOCABULARY
Months and seasons

6 🔊 7.08 **Put the months in the correct order. Write 1–12 in the boxes. Listen and check.**

☐ June	☐ September	☐ April
☐ May	☐ February	☐ December
☐ March	1 January	☐ July
☐ November	☐ August	☐ October

7 In what months are these seasons in your country?

winter

spring

summer

fall

→ workbook page 66

GRAMMAR
Prepositions of time

8 Read the example sentences and complete the rule with *in*, *at*, and *on*.

The soccer game starts **at** 3 p.m.
My birthday is **in** March. It's **in** the spring.
The party is **on** Friday.

> **RULE:** With times, we use [1]____________ .
> For months and seasons, we use [2]____________ .
> For days of the week, we use [3]____________ .

9 🔊 7.09 **Do you know when these sporting events are? Guess, then listen and check.**

The World Cup final is usually in June or July.

~~The World Cup final~~	The Winter Olympics
The World Series	Wimbledon
The Summer Olympics	The Tour de France

→ workbook page 65

VOCABULARY
Ordinal numbers

10 Look at the article on page 70. Complete the sentence with the missing date.

It's February ____________ at Greece Athena High School, New York.

> **Look**
> When we say the date, we usually say **March 7th**, but we write March 7.

11 🔊 7.10 **Match the numbers with the words. Listen, check, and repeat.**

1st ☐	9th ☐	**a** sixth	**i** thirtieth
2nd ☐	10th ☐	**b** eleventh	**j** eighth
3rd ☐	11th ☐	**c** thirteenth	**k** thirty-first
4th ☐	12th ☐	**d** third	**l** twelfth
5th ☐	13th ☐	**e** tenth	**m** second
6th ☐	20th ☐	**f** fifth	**n** twentieth
7th ☐	30th ☐	**g** ninth	**o** seventh
8th ☐	31st ☐	**h** first	**p** fourth

12 SPEAKING **Write three important dates for you. Tell your partner about them.**

My sister's birthday is on May 8th.

Our school's Field Day is on June 20th.

→ workbook page 66

WRITING
My favorite athlete

13 Think of your favorite athlete and answer the questions.

1 Who is he/she?
2 Where is he/she from?
3 What sport does he/she play?
4 What sort of things can he/she do?
5 Are there any things he/she can't do?
6 Why do you like him/her?

14 SPEAKING **Work in pairs. Tell your partner about your favorite athlete.**

15 Write a short text (50–70 words) about your favorite athlete. Use your ideas and answers from Exercises 13 and 14.

DEVELOPING SPEAKING

1 **Look at the photo. What sport are Nina and Dave going to play?**

2 7.11 **Now read and listen to the dialogue. What is the problem?**

Nina: Do we have everything? Tennis rackets, balls …?
Dave: Yes, I think so. And we have some food – sandwiches, fruit, and stuff – and some water.
So, let's go.
Nina: Just a minute! Oh, no! It's raining! Now what do we do?
Dave: You're right. We can't play outside in the rain.
Nina: Why don't we go to the gym in town? They have an indoor court.
Dave: No, it's always very busy. I'm sure we can't play there today.
Nina: Maybe you're right. It's a little expensive, too.
Dave: OK, so we can't play today. It's no big deal. We can play tomorrow, maybe.
Nina: Yes. But I'm a little sad now.
Dave: Me, too. But what can we do? It's raining, and that's that.
Nina: I know! How about watching some old tennis games on the Internet?
Dave: Good idea. I like watching really good players.
Nina: And we can eat our food.
Dave: Let's go and turn the computer on.

3 SPEAKING **Read the dialogue again. Answer the questions with a partner.**
1 What are Dave and Nina taking with them?
2 Why don't they want to play tennis at the gym?
3 How do they feel about not playing tennis?
4 What do they decide to do instead of playing tennis?

Phrases for fluency

4 **Find the expressions 1–4 in the dialogue. Who says them? How do you say them in your language?**
1 … and stuff ________
2 It's no big deal. ________
3 I'm sure … ________
4 Now what …? ________

5 **Put the sentences in the correct order to make a dialogue.**
☐ **Paul** You know, books and things. I need them for school. Now what do I do?
☐ **Paul** With no books? I don't think so!
[1] **Paul** I don't have my school stuff with me.
☐ **Zoe** Oh, it's no big deal. You can go to class without books.
☐ **Zoe** What school stuff?
☐ **Zoe** Oh, I'm sure you can. Come on, we're late.

6 **Complete the dialogues with the expressions from Exercise 4.**
0 A Who is that woman?
B *I'm sure* she's a famous actress. I can't remember her name.
1 A Come to the store with me.
B I can't. I need to do a lot of work at home, cleaning ________ .
2 A My computer is broken.
B But we need the Internet! ________ do we do?
3 A I can use my phone. Oh no, I can't find it.
B ________ You can use my phone.

FUNCTIONS
Making suggestions

KEY LANGUAGE
Let's [go to the park].
How about [playing a game]?
Why don't you / we [watch some TV]?

7 **Complete the suggestions with the words and phrases from the Key Language box.**
1 A I'm bored.
B ________ watching a movie?
2 A There's nothing to do.
B ________ go for a walk?
3 A I'm hungry.
B OK. ________ make some sandwiches.

8 SPEAKING **Work in pairs. Act out the dialogues in Exercise 7.**

9 SPEAKING **Make two new dialogues. Choose from these words for speaker A or use your own ideas.**
- thirsty
- tired
- cold
- hot
- sad

LIFE COMPETENCIES

Sometimes we have ideas about what we want to do, but our plans don't always go right. We need to find ways to be happy and positive even when things go wrong.

1 ▷21 **Watch the vlog. Why isn't Ethan happy today?**

2 ▷21 **Watch the vlog again. Check (✓) the things Ethan wants to do.**

3 **Read the dialogues. Then match the dialogues (1–3) with the photos (A–C).**

1 **Dad** Do you have gymnastics today, Poppy?
Poppy Yes, but my ankle hurts. So I can't go.
Dad Oh no. I know you love gymnastics.
Poppy Yes, I do. But it's no big deal – I can do some exercises with my arms at home.
Dad But that's not the same, is it?
Poppy I know, but I can't do gymnastics today, so I'm happy to do some arm exercises.

2 **Simon** Hey, Elena. How are you?
Elena Not good. We don't have any electricity. No TV, no Internet, nothing. Only my smartphone.
Simon Oh, no. That's not good. Why not come to my place? We can study together.
Elena Study? I don't want to do that!
Simon OK. So, what do you want to do?
Elena I don't know! Nothing.
Simon Well then, I can't help you. Bye, Elena.

3 **Chloe** Is it a good game?
Jason No! It's 4–0 to the other team. This is awful!
Chloe Oh, I'm sorry about that. But …
Jason But what?
Chloe Well, when the game finishes, we can order pizza!
Jason You're right! What kind of pizza do you want?
Chloe Good for you, Jason! Let's get a veggie pizza!

4 SPEAKING **Ask and answer the questions with a partner.**

1 Who is positive from start to finish?
2 Who is not positive at the start, but is positive at the end?
3 Who is not positive from start to finish?

Me and my world

5 **Check (✓) the things you sometimes don't feel positive about. Add one of your own.**

You have a lot of homework. ☐
You have a bad cold. ☐
Your brother/sister is annoying you. ☐
____________________ ☐

6 SPEAKING **Work in pairs. Discuss what you can do to feel more positive about the things in Exercise 5.**

TIPS FOR BEING POSITIVE

- Ask yourself: "Are things really very bad or just not so good?"
- Think about how you can fix the problem.
- Alone, or with another person, try to think of what you can do to feel OK again.

8 FEEL THE RHYTHM

OBJECTIVES

FUNCTIONS: talking about music and feelings; describing a scene; talking about likes and dislikes

GRAMMAR: present continuous; *like / don't like + -ing*

VOCABULARY: clothes

Get THINKING

Watch the video and think: how important is music in your life?

READING

1 **Match the words in the list with the photos. Write 1–4 in the boxes.**

1 a concert | **2** lights | **3** a singer | **4** a stage

2 SPEAKING **Look at the photos on page 75. Do you know the singer? Do you like concerts? Tell your partner.**

3 SPEAKING **What do you know about Twitter? Do you know of any other microblogs? Tell your partner.**

4 8.01 **Read and listen to the microblog and answer the questions.**

0 How does Lucy feel at 5:34?
excited

1 Where is Lucy at 6:50?

2 What is Lucy eating at 7:17?

3 What time does the show start?

4 What is Lucy's favorite Jess Glynne song?

5 How does Lucy feel when she gets home?

6 What time does Lucy go to bed?

#musicintheforest

#Lucybanner

New posts

5:34 I'm leaving home. We're on our way to the station. I'm so excited!

6:05 We're standing on the platform waiting for the train to Delamere Forest.

6:30 We're here. What a great place to see my favorite singer – Jess Glynne – right in the middle of a beautiful forest.

7:17 I'm eating a hot dog. It's very expensive, but it isn't very good!

7:57 It's getting dark now. The stage is completely black. A few people are talking, but most people are quiet. We're waiting for Jess. And here she comes. Everyone is cheering. What a noise!

9:45 Jess isn't on stage. Is the show over? No way. We're all shouting, "More!" Why are we shouting? Because we want MORE!!! But don't worry. She's walking back onto the stage.

10:56 We're on the train home. We aren't sitting down. I don't care. There are so many people on the train and everybody's a Jess Glynne fan. We're all singing "Hold my Hand." It's my favorite song.

12:00 It's exactly midnight and we're back home. I'm tired but very happy. I'm going straight upstairs to bed.

TH!NK values

Music

5 SPEAKING **Work in pairs. Check (✓) the places where you listen to music. Tell your partner. How many are the same?**

in my room	☐	on the bus/train	☐
outside	☐	at the store	☐
at school	☐	another place (where?)	☐

I listen to music in my room, outside, and on the bus.

6 **What are your reasons for listening to music? Write 1–3 in the boxes: 3 = a very important reason, 2 = an important reason, 1 = not an important reason.**

☐ It makes me happy.
☐ I can listen with friends.
☐ It's free.
☐ I can forget my problems.
☐ I can dance to it.

7 SPEAKING **Work in pairs and compare your answers.**

Grammar rap!

GRAMMAR
Present continuous

1 Look at the examples of the present continuous. Find other examples in the microblogs on page 75. Then choose the correct words to complete the rule and the table.

I'**m leaving** home.
We **aren't sitting** down.
Why **are** we **shouting**?

> **RULE:** We use the present continuous to talk about things that [1]*happen every day / are happening now.* We form the present continuous with the present tense of [2]*to be / to have* and the *-ing* form of the main verb.

Positive	Negative	Question + short answer
I'm (am) listening.	I'm not (am not) listening.	[7]__________ I listening? Yes, I [8]__________ . No, I'm not.
You/We/They [3]__________ (are) listening.	You/We/They aren't (are not) [5]__________ .	[9]__________ you/we/they listening? Yes, you/we/they are. No, you/we/they [10]__________ .
He/She/It [4]__________ (is) listening.	He/She/It [6]__________ (is not) listening.	[11]__________ he/she/it [12]__________ ? Yes, he/she/it [13]__________ . No, he/she/it isn't.

2 Look at the pictures. Then write a name to complete the sentences.

0 ___*Lucas*___ is singing.
1 __________ are sitting.
2 __________ is talking on the phone.
3 __________ is leaving.
4 __________ is reading.
5 __________ are dancing.
6 __________ are standing and cheering.
7 __________ is running.
8 __________ is taking a photo.
9 __________ is wearing a skirt.

> **Look**
> Spelling:
> sing – sing**ing** live – liv**ing**
> swim – swimm**ing**

3 Write the correct *-ing* form of these verbs.

0 come ___*coming*___
1 take __________
2 get __________
3 shop __________
4 make __________
5 watch __________
6 play __________
7 study __________

4 Complete the sentences with the verbs from Exercise 3 in the correct form.

0 **A** Come on, Ruth, we're late!
B OK, Liam, I*'m coming* ___ now!
1 **A** Where's Jane?
B She's in her bedroom. She __________ TV.
2 **A** Is Hamid here?
B No, he isn't. He __________ tennis in the park.
3 **A** Can I talk to Bob, please?
B Sorry, he's at the supermarket. He __________ for food.
4 **A** Let's go home now.
B You're right. It __________ late. Look, it's almost 11 o'clock.
5 **A** Is your dad in the kitchen?
B Yes, he is! He __________ a cake!
6 **A** Where's Paul?
B He __________ the dog for a walk in the street.
7 **A** So, your sister is in Australia.
B That's right. She __________ at a university there.

→ workbook page 72

LISTENING

5 **Look at the different musicians in the photos. Say where you think they come from. Choose from the countries in the list.**

Brazil | Burundi | China | Indonesia
Mexico | Scotland | Spain

A

C

B

D

6 **In which photos can you see these things? Write 1–4 in the boxes.**

1 The people are walking and hitting the drums.
2 The men are walking and wearing red and white socks.
3 A man is playing a guitar. He's wearing a big hat.
4 The women are wearing traditional colorful clothes. They are sitting down.

7 8.02 **Listen to the radio program. Which three photos from Exercise 5 do the people talk about?**

8 8.02 **Listen again. Choose the correct options.**

0 Liliana *often* / *sometimes* goes to Mexico.
1 Liliana really likes the *shirts* / *hats* the musicians wear.
2 Lewis thinks that Gamelan sounds *awful* / *beautiful*.
3 The Gamelan musicians wear the *same* / *different* clothes.
4 Jen *likes* / *doesn't usually like* African drumming.
5 The Burundi flag is green, red, and *blue* / *white*.

9 **Imagine you can watch one of the music performances. Which one do you want to watch?**

FUNCTIONS

Describing a scene

10 **Match 1–3 with a–c. When we describe a scene, we often use:**

1 the present continuous ☐
2 prepositions ☐
3 adjectives ☐

a for colors, sizes, etc.
b to say what people are doing.
c to say where people and things are.

11 **Read the text and answer the questions.**

1 Which photo from Exercise 5 is this person describing?
2 Underline examples of the language mentioned in Exercise 10 (present continuous, prepositions, adjectives).

There is a group of men. They are all walking in the street. They are carrying a strange instrument under their arms. They are wearing black jackets and green skirts, called kilts. They are also wearing black hats on their heads. They are playing the instruments. They are very serious.

12 SPEAKING **Look at the picture. Work in pairs. Describe the scene.**

READING

1 **Read the interview. Match the interviewer's questions and comments with Danny's answers.**

1 What do you do?
2 Thanks, Danny, and good luck.
3 What do you like doing in your free time?
4 Who are you?
5 What do you like wearing?
6 Wow. That's interesting. Can you tell us more?

☐ I'm Danny Boyd. I'm 14 years old and I'm from Chicago.

☐ I'm a student at school and on the weekends, I work as a DJ.

☐ I'm a DJ at a local youth club. I play every Saturday from 6 p.m. to 10 p.m.. There's usually about 100 people there. It's a lot of fun. I also sometimes play for big crowds in the park and sometimes at the beach, too.

☐ I love listening to music and finding new songs to play. I like watching movies and playing games on my VR headset. But I hate dancing. I know that's a strange thing for a DJ to say. I love watching other people dance, but I never dance myself!

☐ When I'm DJing, I like wearing jeans and a white T-shirt. I also wear a red cap. I don't like wearing formal shirts and pants.

☐ Thank you! Why don't you come to one of my shows one day?

2 🔊 8.03 **Listen to the interview to check your answers.**

3 **Read the dialogue again and complete the sentences.**

0 Danny Boyd lives *in Chicago.*
1 On the weekends, he ____________
2 He loves music, but he hates ____________
3 He likes wearing ____________

GRAMMAR

like / don't like + -ing

4 **Complete the sentences from the interview. Then complete the rule.**

0 I like *watching* movies.
1 I don't like ____________ shirts and pants.
2 I love ____________ to music.
3 What do you like ____________ ?

> **RULE:** We use the verbs (*don't*) *like* / [4]____________ / *hate* + verb + *-ing* to talk about how we feel about activities.

5 **Write *like*, *don't like*, *love*, and *hate* in the correct places.**

🙂🙂 1 ____________
🙂 2 ____________
🙁 3 ____________
🙁🙁 4 ____________

6 **Complete the sentences. Use a verb from Exercise 5 and the correct form of the verb in parentheses.**

0 I *love watching* sports on TV. 🙂🙂 (watch)
1 I ____________ to the movies. 🙁 (go)
2 I ____________ early. 🙁🙁 (get up)
3 My family ____________ to France on vacation. 🙂 (go)
4 My best friend ____________ . 🙂🙂 (run)
5 My parents ____________ . 🙁 (dance)
6 ____________ your parents ____________ ? 🙂 (cook)
7 ____________ your teacher ____________ homework? 🙂 (give)

7 SPEAKING **Look at the sentences in Exercise 6. Which are true for you? Change the ones that are not true for you. Then tell your partner.**

→ workbook page 73

VOCABULARY
Clothes

8 8.04 **Match the clothes in the list with the pictures. Write 1–12 in the boxes. Listen and check.**

| **1** a coat | **2** a dress | **3** jeans | **4** pants | **5** a shirt | **6** shoes | **7** shorts | **8** skirt | **9** sneakers | **10** socks | **11** a sweater | **12** T-shirt |

9 Look at the pictures in Exercise 8 again. What are the people wearing?

0 Eli is wearing *blue jeans, a white T-shirt, and sneakers.*
1 Beth is wearing ________________ .
2 Jake ________________ .
3 Anisa ________________ .
4 Simon ________________ .

10 SPEAKING **Work in pairs. Ask and answer the questions.**

1 What clothes do you love wearing? What clothes do you hate wearing?
2 Do you like shopping for clothes? Why or why not?
3 What is your teacher wearing today?
4 Which color do you love or hate wearing?

I love wearing jeans and sneakers, but I hate wearing shoes and pants.

→ workbook page 74

PRONUNCIATION
Intonation – listing items Go to page 121.

Train to TH!NK
Memorizing

11 Look at the picture for two minutes.

12 SPEAKING **Student A: Turn to page 127. Student B: Turn to page 128. Listen to the questions your partner asks and answer them with short answers. Correct the negative answers.**

TH!NK

Dances around the world

Culture

DANCES
AROUND THE WORLD

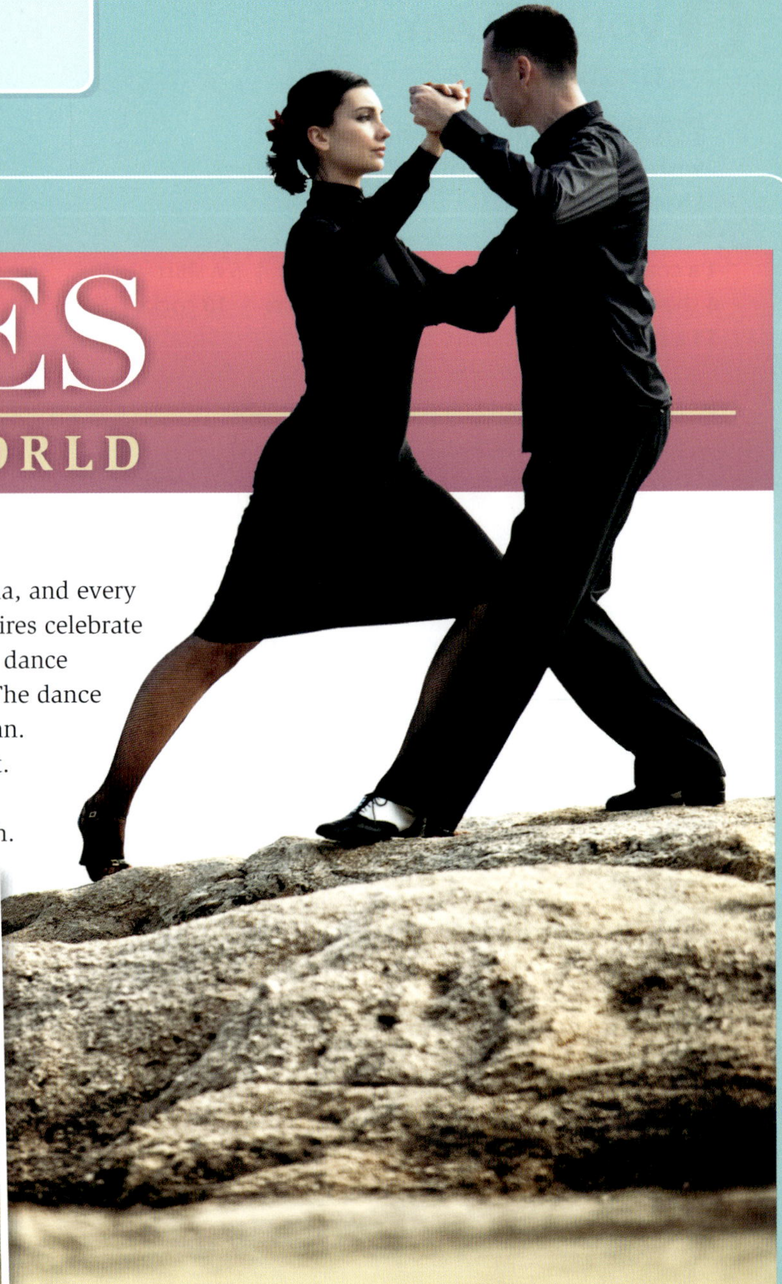

1 THE TANGO

The tango is the national dance of Argentina, and every year on December 11th people in Buenos Aires celebrate the Day of the Tango. They do the tango in dance halls, parks, and squares all over the city. The dance is usually performed by a man and a woman. The man often wears nice pants and a shirt. The woman often wears a beautiful dress. The dance is often very interesting to watch.

2 THE WHIRLING DERVISH

The Whirling Dervish is a dance from Turkey. There is a group of twelve men who dance. They wear traditional costumes with big skirts. They often all wear white, but sometimes the skirts are different colors. There is another group of twelve musicians. They play traditional Turkish instruments. As the music plays, the dancers spin around in circles, getting faster and faster. The dance is very popular with tourists.

3 IRISH DANCING

There are lots of Irish dances, but perhaps the most famous one is the "step dance." One or more dancers perform the step dance. The dancers only move their legs. They move them very quickly. The top half of the body doesn't move. Dancers usually wear traditional Irish costumes. The music they dance to is played by an Irish folk band. They play instruments like the fiddle and the whistle.

1 **Look at the photos on page 80. Find these things and the action.**

a dress | a traditional costume (x2) | curly hair | to spin | nice pants

2 8.07 **Read and listen to the article. Which countries do the dances come from?**

3 **Read the article again. Mark the sentences T (true) or F (false).**

0 December 1st is the National Tango Day in Argentina. F
1 Tango dancers usually wear very nice clothes. ☐
2 Men and women dance the Whirling Dervish. ☐
3 Twenty-four people are involved in a Whirling Dervish performance. ☐
4 The step dance is from Ireland. ☐
5 Step dancers move their whole body. ☐

4 SPEAKING **Are there any special dances in your country? Can you do any of the dances? Discuss with your partner.**

WRITING
Describing a scene

1 INPUT **Read the microblog and look at the photos. Where is Maddie? Check (✓) the correct photo.**

2 ANALYZE **Read the microblog again. Find examples of the present continuous.**

3 PLAN **Write notes to describe how you are feeling in each of these situations.**

1 You're at a bus stop. It's raining. You're going to meet friends to see a local band play. The bus doesn't come.
2 You're at home. You have to study. The weather outside is very nice and you want to go out, but you have to stay inside.
3 You're at home. You're watching a great movie. You want to tell your friends that it's really good.

4 PRODUCE **Use your notes from Exercise 3 to write a microblog for each situation in Exercise 3.**

Remember:

- A microblog message is very short. For example, a Tweet can only be be 280 characters (including spaces).
- Split your microblog into different parts, so you can describe what is happening at different times and how the situation is changing.

New posts Profile

7:22 Here we are. We're waiting. I think there are more than 3,000 people here! It's fantastic. People are singing and smiling – great!

comment Share

7:28 I think they're coming out now. Yes – here they are! Everyone is shouting and cheering!! And the band is smiling. They're very happy.

comment Share

7:49 They're playing my favorite song! I'm so happy and my friends are smiling and singing. I'm watching my favorite band – this is the best!

comment Share

A

B

TOWARDS A2 Key for Schools

LISTENING

3-option multiple choice

1 8.08 **You will hear five short conversations. There is one question for each conversation. For each question choose the right answer (A, B or C).**

1 What time does Bob get home from school?

A ☐ B ☐ C ☐

2 When is Sue's birthday?

A ☐ B ☐ C ☐

3 What is Lucy's favourite month?

A ☐ B ☐ C ☐

4 Which instrument does Mike play?

A ☐ B ☐ C ☐

5 Which of Jenny's clothes does Liam like?

A ☐ B ☐ C ☐

READING AND WRITING

Open cloze

2 **Write ONE word in each space to complete the text.**

Joaquim

Hi Sylvie,

I'm sorry, but I [0] ___*can't*___ come to your place tonight. It's the big match tonight and I want [1] __________ watch it on TV. I know you've [2] __________ a TV, too, but I really want to watch the game with my dad. He's a big football fan, [3] __________ mum isn't, and dad [4] __________ like watching sport on TV alone.

I hope that's OK – please don't be angry with me! Let's go cycling together [5] __________ Sunday – I'll call you.

See you,

Joaquim

TEST YOURSELF UNITS 7 & 8

VOCABULARY

1 Complete the sentences with the words in the list. There are two extra words.

cheering | coat | doing | making | sitting | sneakers | studying | surf | taking | third | three | volleyball

1 It's cold outside. Put a ______________________ on when you go out.
2 I love playing ______________________ .
3 We like ______________________ in the park on hot summer days.
4 I'm in the kitchen. I'm ______________________ pizzas for the party.
5 My brother is in Canada. He's ______________________ French at a university there.
6 You can't wear ______________________ to a party! Wear your new shoes.
7 My brother's at the gym. He's ______________________ Taekwondo.
8 I love ______________________ photos of different sports.
9 My birthday? It's on the ______________________ of January.
10 They're winning! Everyone is ______________________ !

/10

GRAMMAR

2 Complete the sentences with the words in the list.

can | can't | don't | like | stand | standing

1 Do you ______________________ reading magazines?
2 I don't like ______________________ on the train.
3 I'm sick. I ______________________ go out today.
4 I don't want to sit down. I can ______________________ and watch. It's OK.
5 We really ______________________ like going surfing in the winter.
6 He ______________________ run 400 meters in 70 seconds.

3 Find and correct the mistake in each sentence.

1 He can to count to 20 in Spanish.
2 Please be quiet. I'm study for the test next Monday.
3 He doesn't can speak German.
4 I don't like play tennis.
5 She's downtown right now. She shops.
6 Does she can play the piano?

/12

FUNCTIONAL LANGUAGE

4 Write the missing words.

don't | how | let's | o'clock | time | to | wearing | what's

1 A ______________________ the time?
B It's four ______________________ . I'm bored!
A Me, too. Why ______________________ we play a game?
B A game? No thanks. ______________________ about going cycling?

2 A Look at those people! They're ______________________ very strange clothes.
B Yes, they're going to a big party in the park. It's a holiday today!
A What ______________________ does the party start?
B At three o'clock. Oh, look! It's a quarter ______________________ three now!
______________________ go and join them.

/8

MY SCORE /30

22–30 | 10–21 | 0–9

9 WHO'S HUNGRY?

OBJECTIVES

FUNCTIONS:
talking about food and eating habits; talking about obligation; asking nicely and offering; offering and asking for help

GRAMMAR:
must / mustn't; can (asking for permission); *I'd like … / Would you like …?*

VOCABULARY:
food and drink; meals

Get THINKING

Watch the video and think: what is your favorite food?

READING

1 **Match the words in the list with the photos. Write 1–6 in the boxes.**

1 carrot cake | 2 a chef | 3 an omelet
4 some salad | 5 steak | 6 tomato soup

2 SPEAKING **Work in pairs. What other food words do you know?**

pizza, apples, hamburgers, …

3 SPEAKING **Tell your partner what food you like and don't like.**

I like … I don't like …

4 **Look at the photos on page 85. What is unusual about the chefs? Read the article quickly and check your ideas.**

5 9.01 **Read and listen to the article again. Mark the sentences T (true), F (false), or DS (doesn't say).**

0 Harry wants to be a star chef. *T*
1 He is ten years old and he's from New York. ____
2 His sister likes cooking, too, but she's not very good. ____
3 The other children on the TV show aren't very good cooks. ____
4 Children must be ten years old to be on *Kitchen Kids*. ____
5 The chefs' hands must be clean. ____
6 It's OK for the children to eat the food they are cooking. ____
7 After the TV show, Harry goes home to study. ____

KITCHEN KIDS

Harry doesn't want to be a star chef when he's 20. He wants to be one now. This is why he's on the TV show *Kitchen Kids*.

The ten-year-old New Yorker likes cooking. He can make fantastic soups and salads, excellent omelets, and the best cakes. But there are many other children on the show, too. And they are all very good.

More and more young people are interested in cooking. Many of them learn it from their parents. Others watch special cooking videos for children on YouTube©. In many cities, there are special cooking classes for young people. Some of them are for three-year-olds!

But what must you do to become a star chef? Of course, it's important that you like cooking and are really good at it. But there are some rules. You must be nine years old or older to be on *Kitchen Kids*.

"We must wash our hands before we start cooking," Harry says. "And of course we mustn't put them in our mouths. A chef doesn't do that! And we must be very careful with hot plates."

The show starts. Harry is excited. He knows he's an excellent cook. This time he makes tomato soup, some salad, steak, and carrot cake. The experts in the studio love Harry's food and he stays on the show.

It's 5 p.m. The show is over. Harry is happy and a little tired. He goes home. It's time to do his homework.

THINK values

How you eat is important

6 SPEAKING **How often do you do these things? Write *always, sometimes, often,* or *never*. Then tell the class.**

- ☐ a sit at a table to eat ________
- ☐ b eat alone ________
- ☐ c eat slowly ________
- ☐ d eat very fast ________
- ☐ e eat with other people ________
- ☐ f eat and play computer games at the same time ________

I always eat slowly. I sometimes eat with other people.

7 **Look again at the things in Exercise 6. Are they good things to do? Write 1–3 in the boxes: 1 = a good thing to do, 2 = an OK thing to do, 3 = a bad thing to do.**

8 SPEAKING **Work in pairs and compare your ideas.**

I often eat ...

I think ... is good.

I think ... is not so good.

GRAMMAR
must / *mustn't*

1 Look at the article on page 85. Complete the sentences with *must* or *mustn't*. Then complete the rule.

1 You ____________ be nine years old or older to be on *Kitchen Kids*.
2 We ____________ wash our hands before we start cooking.
3 We ____________ put them in our mouths.

> **RULE:** We use *must* and *mustn't* to talk about rules.
> Use [4]____________ to say that it's necessary to do something.
> Use [5]____________ to say that it's not OK to do something.

Meat

0 *chicken* 1 ________ 2 ________ 3 ________

Fruit

4 ________ 5 ________ 6 ________ 7 ________

Vegetables

8 ________ 9 ________ 10 ________ 11 ________

Drinks

12 ________ 13 ________ 14 ________ 15 ________

2 Complete the dialogues. Use *must* or *mustn't* and a verb from the list.

buy | eat | forget | go

0 A Jake has a new cat.
B Oh, really. We *must go* and see it.
1 A Mom, can I have some ice cream?
B Of course not! You know you ____________ ice cream before lunch.
2 A Hey, can I read that book?
B Sure, but you ____________ to give it back. It's my brother's.
3 A Oh, no. There isn't any cheese.
B I ____________ some for the spaghetti bolognese.

3 SPEAKING Work in pairs. Think of some things that are important for you to do (or not do) in the next few days.

I must call my grandma.

I mustn't forget to finish my history project.

→ workbook page 82

VOCABULARY
Food and drink

4 🔊 9.02 Write the names of the food and drinks under the photos. Listen and check.

5 SPEAKING Work in pairs. Say which word in each group is different. Why?

0 coffee – (potato) – tea
1 banana – orange – hamburger
2 carrot – chicken – beef
3 milk – strawberry – apple
4 pepper – potato – orange juice

Number 0 is potato – coffee and tea are drinks.

6 SPEAKING Look again at the food words in Exercise 4. Work in pairs. Ask and answer questions to find three things you both like.

Do you like strawberries?

Yes, I love them. And you?

I like them. Do you like ...?

→ workbook page 84

LISTENING

7 **Look at the photo. What can you see?**

8 9.03 **Listen to the dialogue. What do they decide to eat in the end?**

9 9.03 **Listen again. Put the sentences in the order you hear them. Write 1–6 in the boxes.**

- [ ] **a** Can we do that later?
- [1] **b** Can we make some sandwiches, Dad?
- [ ] **c** Can we use this cheese, Dad?
- [ ] **d** There are some tomatoes.
- [ ] **e** Would you like some help?
- [ ] **f** Can we go out for pizza, Dad?

GRAMMAR

can (asking for permission)

10 **Match these answers to the questions in Exercise 9. Then read the rule.**

1 Hmm ... OK. Yes, we can. [ ]
2 No, we can't. [ ]
3 No. Your mom wants that for the lasagna. [ ]

> **RULE:** We use *can* + subject to ask if it's OK to do something.

11 9.04 **Complete the questions with *can* and a verb from the list. Listen and check.**

~~do~~ | eat | go out | play | try on | use

0 *Can* I *do* my homework later?
1 ________ I ________ these jeans, please?
2 ________ I ________ your laptop, please?
3 Dad, ________ I ________ tonight?
4 ________ we ________ soccer in the yard?
5 ________ we ________ dinner in front of the TV?

12 **Match the answers with the questions in Exercise 11.**

- [0] **a** No, you can't. Do it now.
- [ ] **b** Of course you can. But be careful.
- [ ] **c** No, you can't. You have school tomorrow.
- [ ] **d** Sorry, I need it to write some emails.
- [ ] **e** Yes, the changing room is over there.
- [ ] **f** Well, OK ... , it's your birthday.

→ workbook page 82

SPEAKING

13 **Think about what is true for you. Choose 1–5 (1 = strongly agree, 5 = strongly disagree).**

1 I often eat between meals. 1 – 2 – 3 – 4 – 5
2 I always eat breakfast. 1 – 2 – 3 – 4 – 5
3 I eat fruit and vegetables every day. 1 – 2 – 3 – 4 – 5
4 I drink lots of water. 1 – 2 – 3 – 4 – 5
5 I eat lots of candy. 1 – 2 – 3 – 4 – 5
6 I brush my teeth after every meal. 1 – 2 – 3 – 4 – 5

14 **Work in pairs. Compare your answers with a partner.**

I often eat between meals.

I eat fruit every day.

15 **Discuss your answers with the rest of the class. Does everyone have the same answers?**

READING

1 **Read the menu. What food on it would you like?**

2 9.05 **Read and listen to the dialogue. What does Emma eat? What does Oscar eat?**

Server Hello. Can I help you?
Emma Hi. Yes, we'd like a table for two, please.
Server Here are the menus.
Oscar Thanks.
Server What would you like to drink?
Emma I'd like an orange juice.
Oscar And I'd like water, please.
Server Great.
(Two minutes later ...)
Server Are you ready to order now?
Emma Yes, I'd like the pizza with salad.
Server Any starters?
Emma No, thanks.
Server Would you like any extra toppings on the pizza? Onion, peppers, or tomatoes?
Emma Some peppers, please.
Server And what would you like?
Oscar I'd like the chicken and fries.
Server OK. Is that everything?
Oscar Yes, thank you.
(Half an hour later ...)
Server Would you like a dessert?
Oscar Yes, please. I'd like the fruit salad with vanilla ice cream.
Emma Me, too.
(Ten minutes later ...)
Server How are your desserts?
Oscar Great.
Server Would you like any more drinks?
Emma No, thanks. We'd like the check, please.
Server Of course.

Apple Tree CAFÉ

MENU

OUR STARTERS

Watermelon and cheese salad **$5.25**
Salad (tuna fish and tomato) **$7.50**
Tomato soup **$6.60**

OUR MAIN COURSES

Four-cheese pizza **$9.50**
(extra toppings – onion, peppers, tomatoes)
Pasta with tomato sauce **$8.50**
Turkey sandwich **$8.50**
Chicken and fries **$7.80**
Cheese and tomato sandwich **$6.50**
Baked potato **$5.20**

OUR DESSERTS

Fruit salad **$2.40**
banana, strawberry, mango, apple, and grapes
Ice cream (per scoop) **$1.20**
Vanilla, strawberry, lemon, and chocolate
Chocolate pudding **$1.20**

OUR DRINKS

Fruit juice (orange or apple) **$1.90**
Coffee **$2.20**
Tea **$1.60**
Hot chocolate **$2.10**
Water **$1.10**

3 **Who says these things in a restaurant? Write S (server) or C (customer) in the boxes.**

0 Can I help you? [S]
1 A table for two, please. [ ]
2 Here are the menus. [ ]
3 Are you ready to order? [ ]
4 I'd like the vegetable soup. [ ]
5 What would you like to drink? [ ]
6 Can we have the check, please? [ ]
7 Would you like dessert? [ ]

4 SPEAKING **Work in pairs. Look again at the menu and think of more food to add.**

GRAMMAR
I'd like ... / Would you like ...?

5 **Complete these sentences from the dialogue on page 88. Then complete the rule.**

1 And what ___________ you like?
2 ___________ like the chicken and fries.
3 Would you ___________ a dessert?
4 ___________ like the check, please.

> **RULE:** We use *I + would ('d)* + [5]___________ to ask for something in a nice way.
> We use *Would + you* + [6]___________ ... ? to offer something.

6 **How do you say *Would you like ...?* and *I'd like ...* in your language?**

7 **Put the words in the correct order to make sentences or questions.**

0 like / a / I'd / please / banana, / .
I'd like a banana, please.
1 like / some / you / Would / coffee / ?
____
2 a / like / turkey / I'd /, please / sandwich / .
____
3 you / What / to / would / like / eat / ?
____
4 to / We'd / like / here / sit / .
____
5 would / this afternoon / What / you / to / like / do / ?
____

8 **Complete these sentences.**

1 ___________ to order now?
2 ___________ some coffee?
3 We ___________ to sit there, please.
4 I ___________ some ice cream, please.

9 SPEAKING **Work in groups. One of you is the server at the Apple Tree Café, the others order food and drinks. Act out the situation. Then switch roles.**

→ workbook page 83

PRONUNCIATION
Intonation – giving two choices Go to page 121.

VOCABULARY
Meals

10 9.08 **Match the words in the list to the items in the picture. Write 1–9 in the boxes. Listen and check.**

1 bread | 2 butter | 3 cereal | 4 egg | 5 fruit
6 honey | 7 jelly | 8 toast | 9 yogurt

11 SPEAKING **Copy the table into your notebook and complete it. Then tell the class.**

	always	often	sometimes	never
breakfast				
lunch				
dinner				

For breakfast, I always drink ...

I never have (any) ... for lunch.

→ workbook page 84

WRITING
A meal plan for your friend

12 **Ask a partner to give you his/her table from Exercise 11. Imagine he/she is staying at your house for two days. You want to make meals that he/she likes. Write a menu for your partner for both days.**

SATURDAY		SUNDAY	
	Breakfast:		Breakfast:
	Lunch:		Lunch:
	Dinner:		Dinner:

13 SPEAKING **Show your ideas to your partner. Is he/she happy with the meals?**

DEVELOPING SPEAKING

1 **Look at the photo. What is Jo doing?**

2 9.09 **Now read and listen to the dialogue. What happens to Jo's lasagna?**

Mom: Wow! What a great smell!
Jo: Thanks, Mom. It's lasagna. It's in the oven and it's almost ready.
Mom: Lasagna from the store?
Jo: No, Mom, it's my lasagna. It's got meat, pepper, mushrooms, cheese, onion – everything. And we can eat it with a little salad.
Mom: Oh, right. But, we? Who's coming for lunch?
Jo: Mark and Chloe. We want to study together this afternoon and have lunch together first. That's OK, right?
Mom: Of course, Jo. But ...
Jo: But what, Mom?
Mom: Well, the thing is, I'd like a nice, quiet afternoon.
Jo: Oh, don't worry, Mom. After lunch, we plan to study upstairs in my room.
Jo: Ah! It's ready.
Mom: Be careful, Jo. It's very hot. Can I help you?
Jo: It's OK, Mom. I can just ... Oh, no! My lasagna! It's all over the floor. Now what?
Mom: Well, first, let's clean it all up. And then ... do you and your friends want to go to the new sandwich place?
Jo: Not really. But I have an idea, Mom. We can just have the salad!
Mom: OK. And you and I can make some chocolate-covered bananas, so your friends can have some dessert, too.
Jo: Thanks, Mom, you're the best!

3 SPEAKING **Read the dialogue again. Answer the questions with a partner.**

1 Who cooked the lasagna?
2 Who is coming to have lunch with Jo?
3 What does Jo's mom want this afternoon?
4 What can Jo do to fix the problem?

Phrases for fluency

4 **Find the expressions 1–4 in the dialogue. Who says them? How do you say them in your language?**

1 Of course. ____________
2 Be careful ... ____________
3 a little ... ____________
4 the thing is, ... ____________

5 **Put the sentences in the correct order to make a dialogue.**

☐ **Harry** Well, the thing is, I want to cook some Indian food.
1 **Harry** Do you like Indian food?
☐ **Harry** Yes, but I don't know how to cook.
☐ **Claire** Oh. And you need a little help.
☐ **Claire** Of course. I love curry and stuff. Why?
☐ **Claire** OK. You can use my mom's cookbook. But be careful! She loves that book!

6 **Complete the dialogues with the expressions from Exercise 4.**

1 **A** Let's go to the movies tonight.
B No thanks. I have [1]____________ work to do.
A Really? On Saturday?
B No, not really. I'm sorry. [2]____________, I don't have any money.

2 **A** Can I look at your new phone?
B [3]____________. Here it is.
A Oh, it's really nice!
B Thanks, I love it. Oh, [4]____________! Don't break it!

FUNCTIONS
Offering and asking for help

KEY LANGUAGE

Can you ...?	Do you want ...?
Can I ...?	Thank you. / No, thank you.

7 **Complete the dialogues using the phrases from the Key Language box.**

A [1]____________ help me for a moment?
B Of course. What would you like me to do?
A [2]____________. I need some help cleaning the kitchen.
A [3]____________ help you with anything?
B [4]____________. I'm OK.

8 **Work in pairs. Think of a situation where you would ask for or offer help. Write a dialogue. Use phrases from the Key Language box.**

9 SPEAKING **Act out your dialogues from Exercise 8.**

LIFE COMPETENCIES

We all want to do the things that we want to do – it makes us feel good. But thinking about other people, helping them, and making them happy can make us feel good, too.

1 ▶27 **Watch the vlog. Why can't Becky eat the pizza?**

2 ▶27 **Watch the vlog again. Match the food to the people in Becky's family.**

A

____

B

____

C

____

3 **Read the dialogues. Who do you think says these things?**

1 What a nice party.
2 Thanks for dinner, guys.

Mike I'm hungry. Let's call and get some Indian food.
Emma Curry! Yes! That's a great idea.
Mike Oh, just a minute. The thing is, Peter doesn't like Indian food very much.
Emma Oh, don't worry, he'll be OK with a curry.
Mike No, I don't think so. Let's get pizza. He likes pizza.
Emma Well, yes, OK. Pizza's good, too. Where's the phone?

Olivia What are you doing?
Laura I'm choosing the music for the family party.
Olivia Cool. Is *What a Wonderful World* on the list?
Laura Of course not! It's old!
Olivia But Grandma and Grandpa are coming to the party and it's their favorite song.
Laura Oh, yes. You're right. OK, where can I find it?

4 SPEAKING **Ask and answer the questions with a partner.**

1 Who is thinking about other people?
2 What do they decide to do?

Me and my world

5 SPEAKING **How can you show these people you are thinking about them?**

1 Your dad is traveling a lot for work.
2 Your brother is studying hard for some important exams.
3 Your best friend has a broken leg and is in bed for three weeks.

6 SPEAKING **How does it feel when someone thinks about you? Tell your partner.**

TIPS FOR THINKING ABOUT OTHER PEOPLE

- Think about how your actions can change other people's feelings.
- Remember to ask how other people feel.
- Ask yourself: "Does this person need help?" or "Is what I am doing OK for them, too?"

10 BIG SUCCESSES

Get THINKING

Watch the video and think: when do you feel proud of yourself?

OBJECTIVES

FUNCTIONS: talking about achievements; talking about the past; asking for information about the past; talking about the weather

GRAMMAR: simple past: *was / wasn't, were / weren't, there was / were*; simple past: *Was he …? / Were you …?*; simple past: regular verbs

VOCABULARY: time expressions: past; the weather

READING

1 **Match the words in the list with the photos. Write 1–6 in the boxes.**

1 astronaut | 2 competition | 3 factory
4 skydiving | 5 spaceship | 6 stamps

2 SPEAKING **Look at the photos and answer the questions.**

1 What are the names of the two people?
2 Where were they from?
3 Why are they famous?

3 SPEAKING **Name some famous people in your country. Why are they famous?**

… is really famous in our country.

That's true! It's because …

4 10.01 **Read and listen to the article and answer the question.**

Why is Valentina Tereshkova famous?

5 **Read the article again and put the events in order.**

a She was named "Woman of the Century." ☐
b Tereshkova was in space for three days. ☐
c She was the carrier of the Olympic flag. ☐
d There was a competition to find new astronauts. ☐
e Valentina Tereshkova was born. ☐
f She was in a training program. ☐

SHE WAS THE FIRST WOMAN IN SPACE

Posted May 26th

Valentina Tereshkova was born in Russia on March 6, 1937. Her father was a driver and her mother was a factory worker. Valentina was a worker in a factory, too. Her hobby was skydiving and it was her dream to be an astronaut and to go into space.

In 1962, there was a big competition to find new astronauts. There were 400 people interested in going to space. The training program wasn't very easy, but Tereshkova was hard-working. And she was lucky. Tereshkova's big day was June 16, 1963 and she was ready.

The name of her spaceship was Vostok 6 and Tereshkova was the first woman in space. The flight was very difficult because there were many technical problems and Tereshkova was sick for most of the flight. She was in space for three days. She is the only woman to fly into space alone. After that, she was very famous all over the world. Her face was on stamps in many countries.

In the year 2000, there was a big celebration in London and Valentina Tereshkova was named the "Woman of the Century."

At the opening ceremony of the Winter Olympics in Russia in 2014, Valentina Tereshkova was one of the carriers of the Olympic flag.

These were very important moments for her.

TH!NK values

Hard work and achievement

6 **In 2000, Valentina Tereshkova was named "Woman of the Century." Which of the following, do you think, were important for her success? Write N (not important) or I (important).**

1 She was born in 1937. ☐
2 Her mother was a factory worker. ☐
3 Her hobby was skydiving. ☐
4 It was her dream to be an astronaut and go into space. ☐
5 She was hard-working in the training program. ☐
6 The name of her spacecraft was Vostok 6. ☐
7 The flight was difficult, but Tereshkova was strong. ☐
8 She was in space for three days. ☐

7 SPEAKING **Work in pairs and compare your answers. Do you agree?**

She was born in 1937. I think that was important for her success because it was the start of space travel.

I agree. / I don't agree. I think ...

GRAMMAR
Simple past: *was / wasn't; were / weren't; there was / were*

1 Complete the sentences from the article on page 93. Then complete the rule and the table.

1 Valentina Tereshkova ___________ born on March 6, 1937.
2 The training program ___________ very easy.
3 There ___________ 400 people interested in going to space.
4 These ___________ very important moments for her.

RULE: *was/were* is the past form of [5]___________ .

Positive	Negative
I/he/she/it [6]___________ .	I/he/she/it wasn't (was not).
We/you/they were.	We/you/they [8]___________ (were not).
There was / [7]___________ .	There [9]___________ / weren't.

2 Complete the sentences with *was, wasn't, were,* or *weren't.*

1 My friends and I [0]___*were*___ in the park last Sunday. My brother [1]___________ there, too, but my parents [2]___________ there because they [3]___________ at the movies.
2 There [4]___________ lots of people in the park. There [5]___________ a boy with his grandparents. They [6]___________ nice people. The boy's name [7]___________ Greg.

→ workbook page 90

VOCABULARY
Time expressions: past

3 🔊 10.02 **Write *at, in, last,* and *yesterday* to complete the time expressions. Listen and check.**

1 ___________ weekend / Sunday / night / week / month / year
2 ___________ morning / afternoon / evening
3 ___________ 2014
4 ___________ four o'clock / 5:30 / 6 a.m. / 6 p.m.

4 Look at the pictures. Write sentences to say where the people were and when. Use *at, in, last,* or *yesterday*.

at the bookstore | in Rome | in the park | at a birthday party
at the shopping mall | at his friends' house

Eliza was at the shopping mall at ten yesterday morning.

5 Make notes about where you were yesterday at the times in the pictures A–D in Exercise 4.

6 SPEAKING **Work in pairs. Tell your partner where you were yesterday.**

I was downtown at ten yesterday morning. What about you?

I was at home.

7 SPEAKING **Use the information about your partner to report to the class.**

Yesterday morning, Maria was at home. At three thirty yesterday afternoon, she was at a friend's house. In the evening, she was at her grandma's house.

→ workbook page 92

LISTENING

8 **Look at the picture. Where was Alice yesterday? Why wasn't Will there?**

9 10.03 **Listen to the dialogue and check your ideas.**

10 10.03 **Listen again. Match the questions with the answers.**

0 Does Alice say the awards ceremony was good? *e*
1 Were there many parents there? ☐
2 Was Tom Hammond the best student of the year? ☐
3 Who was the best athlete of the year? ☐
4 What was Alice's prize? ☐
5 How does Will feel about Alice? ☐

a No, there weren't.
b It was Tom Hammond.
c He's proud of her.
d No, it was his sister, Sandra.
e No, she says it wasn't.
f A book about science.

GRAMMAR

Simple past: *Was he …? / Were you …?*

11 **Put the words in the correct order to make questions.**

1 the teachers / all / Were / there / ?
____

2 she / last year / Was / the best student / ?
____

3 nice / the / Was / prize / ?
____

12 **Match the answers below with the questions in Exercise 11. Then complete the table.**

a Yes, it was. ☐
b No, she wasn't. ☐
c No, they weren't. ☐

Question	Short answer
Was I/he/she/it … ? [1] ____________ we/ you/they … ?	Yes, I/he/she was. No, I/he/she [2] ____________ . Yes, we/you/they [3] ____________ . No, we/you/they weren't.

13 10.04 **Complete the dialogue with *was, were, wasn't,* or *weren't*. Then listen and check.**

Fiona Oh, no!
Raj What's the matter?
Fiona My phone? Where is it? It [0] *was* in my jacket!
Raj OK, calm down. Where [1] ____________ your phone this morning?
Fiona Well, I [2] ____________ at home from nine o'clock to ten o'clock.
Raj And then? [3] ____________ you in town?
Fiona Yes, I [4] ____________ . I [5] ____________ in the shopping mall. And I'm 100% sure that my phone [6] ____________ in my pocket.
Raj [7] ____________ Steve and Maisie with you?
Fiona No, they [8] ____________ . I [9] ____________ in the shoe store. I bought some new shoes.
Raj Wait a minute. Let me call you.
Fiona It's ringing! Oh, look! It's in the shoe bag! It [10] ____________ there all the time!

→ workbook page 90

FUNCTIONS

Asking for information about the past

14 **Write *was* or *were* to complete the questions. Then ask and answer the questions with a partner. Check your answers on page 93.**

1 ____________ Valentina Tereshkova born in Russia?
2 ____________ her parents astronauts, too?
3 ____________ there 400 people interested in the competition?
4 ____________ the flight very easy or very difficult?
5 ____________ the Winter Olympics in Russia in 2015?

15 **Make notes to answer the following questions.**

1 Where were you at 3 p.m. on Saturday?
2 What was your hobby when you were eight?
3 How old were you in May 2019?
4 How old was your best friend last year?

16 SPEAKING **Work in pairs. Ask and answer the questions in Exercise 15.**

READING

1 Look at the photos of people doing difficult things. Which ones do you think are easy? Hard? Fun?

I think photo 1 is ...

Maybe photo 2 is ...

2 10.05 Read and listen to the comments. Write the correct name beside the photos.

SPORTS ACHIEVERS

Yesterday, I was online and I learned about a woman named Amy who walked all around the UK to get money for charity. And in the winter! When there was rain and snow! Do you know any other amazing stories like that?

A ___________

Jenny *(Five minutes ago)*
How about Dee Caffari? She sailed around the world, non-stop, three times! That's right, three times. Imagine the wind and the rain! Amazing!

B ___________

Sam *(20 minutes ago)*
OK, well there's a boy named Jordan Romero, from the US – he climbed Mount Everest when he was 13 years old. It's really cold up there, but he managed to get to the top. Only 13! Now that's an achievement.

C ___________

Martha *(25 minutes ago)*
My friend Corey Armstrong decided to run a marathon when he was 16. He finished in just over four hours. He enjoyed it a lot, so then he decided to do the marathon in Death Valley in the US. It's so hot there – often more than 40 degrees Celsius. This time he was slower, almost five hours – but I still think it's fantastic. 42 km when it's over 40 degrees! I think he almost died!

D ___________

Mark *(32 minutes ago)*
Before 1926, a lot of women tried to swim the cold water of the English Channel from England to France – but they all failed. But in 1926, Gertrude Ederle (an Olympic gold medal swimmer) arrived on an English beach after 14 hours and 31 minutes. She returned to her home in New York a hero! How about that!?

E ___________

3 Read the comments again. Mark the sentences T (true) or F (false).

0 Dee Caffari sailed around the world alone. [T]
1 She sailed around the world four times. [ ]
2 Jordan Romero was 13 when he climbed Mount Everest. [ ]
3 Corey Armstrong finished his first marathon in 3 hours 50 minutes. [ ]
4 He finished the Death Valley marathon in the same time. [ ]
5 Gertrude Ederle was the first woman to try to swim the English Channel. [ ]
6 Gertrude's cross-channel swim was from France to England. [ ]

4 SPEAKING Do you know any amazing sports achievers? Tell your partner.

Train to TH!NK

Sequencing

5 Put the sentences in order to tell Girl Hero's story.

[ ] There was a very fast car on the road.
[8] Everyone was very happy.
[ ] There were also two young boys in the road.
[1] It was a hot day and Girl Hero wanted an ice cream.
[ ] She walked to an ice cream shop.
[ ] Girl Hero jumped in front of the car and stopped it with her hand.
[ ] She saved the boys.
[ ] She walked out of the shop with her ice cream.

6 SPEAKING Work in pairs. Tell the story. Can you include these lines?

She walked back home.

Girl Hero started to run.

The boys smiled.

GRAMMAR
Simple past: regular verbs

7 **Write the base form of the verbs.**

Base form	0 *finish*	1 ______	2 ______	3 ______
Simple past	finished	sailed	decided	tried

8 **Complete the sentences from the text on page 96 with the past forms from Exercise 7. Then complete the rule.**

1 Dee Caffari ____________ around the world three times.
2 My friend Corey ____________ to run a marathon when he was 16.
3 He ____________ in just over four hours.
4 A lot of women ____________ to swim across the English Channel.

> **RULE:** To form the simple past of regular verbs, add [5]____________ to the base form.
> When the verb ends in *-e*, add *-d*.
> When the verb ends in consonant + *-y*, change *y* to [6]____________ and add *-ed*.

9 **Write the simple past forms of these verbs. Check your answers in the text on page 96.**

1 learn ____________	4 die ____________
2 walk ____________	5 try ____________
3 climb ____________	6 arrive ____________

10 **Complete the text about Simone Biles. Use the simple past form of the verbs in parentheses.**

SIMONE BILES

Simone Biles was born in 1997. When she was six, she [0]*visited* a gym and she [1]__________ (try) gymnastics for the first time. She [2]__________ (love) it! She [3]__________ (join) the gym and [4]__________ (work) hard to become a great gymnast.
In 2013, at the World Championships, she [5]__________ (invent) a new move and now the move is called "the Biles."
In the 2016 Olympics, she [6]__________ (finish) first in five events and won four gold medals. She also [7]__________ (carry) the US flag at the closing ceremony.

→ workbook page 91

PRONUNCIATION
Simple past regular verbs Go to page 121.

VOCABULARY
The weather

11 10.08 **Match the sentences in the list with the pictures. Write 1–8 in the boxes. Listen and check.**

1 It's cloudy. | **2** It's cold. | **3** It's hot.
4 It's raining. | **5** It's snowing.
6 It's sunny. | **7** It's warm. | **8** It's windy.

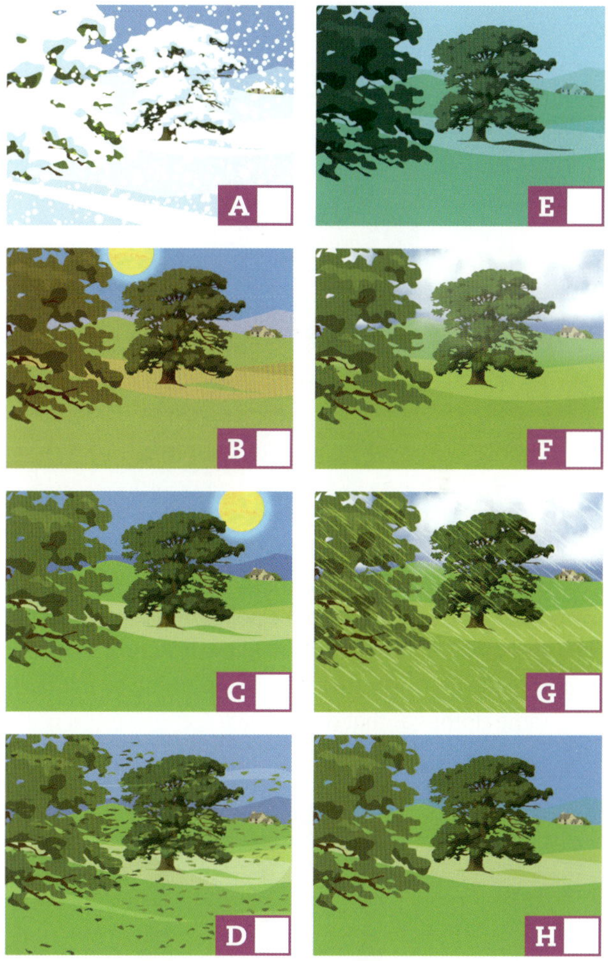

12 **Complete the dialogues with some of the phrases from Exercise 11. Sometimes there is more than one correct answer.**

0 **A** What's the weather like?
B *It's raining*. Take an umbrella.
1 **A** Bye, Mom.
B Bye. But you don't need a sweater. ____________ outside.
2 **A** Hey look! ____________!
B Great! We can go skiing later!
3 **A** Wow, ____________ today.
B I know! Hold on to your hat!

13 SPEAKING **Work in pairs. Write similar dialogues and act them out.**

→ workbook page 92

TH!NK

Statues around the world

Culture

STATUES

There are many wonderful statues all over the world. Many of them help us to remember the lives of great people.

ROSA PARKS

One day in 1965, a bus driver in Alabama, in the US, asked Rosa Parks to give a man her seat – because he was white and she was black. She said "no," and the police decided to take her away. It was a very important moment in the history of black people's rights in the US. The statue shows Rosa sitting on a rock, wearing the same clothes as that day in 1965.

FRANZ KAFKA

Franz Kafka was a writer from Prague. He was born in 1883. His books were in German. During his life, he was not very famous, but now he is. Many of his stories were very strange. There's a very unusual statue of him in Prague. He's sitting on the shoulders of an empty suit!

"OS CANDANGOS"

The "Candangos" were men who traveled from all over Brazil, between 1956 and 1960, to build the new capital city of Brazil, Brasilia. In 1956, 256 men arrived – but before long, there were 30,000, who worked hard to build the city. Brasilia opened in 1960 and this eight-meter-high statue to remember the "Candangos" is in the "Three Powers" square. The two figures are holding digging tools.

SUZANNE LENGLEN

At the Roland Garros tennis center in Paris, there is a court named after Suzanne Lenglen. Lenglen was a famous French tennis player who played from 1914 to 1926. She was the Number One player for many years. In front of the court is this statue: Lenglen is jumping with a racket in her hand and she is wearing her famous white dress and headband.

1 **Look at the photos on page 98. Find these things.**

headband | rock
shoulders | suit | tools

2 10.09 **Read and listen to the article. In which city are the statues of Franz Kafka and Suzanne Lenglen?**

3 **Read the article again. Mark the sentences T (true) or F (false).**

0 Rosa Parks was a black American woman. [T]
1 The police took away the man who wanted Rosa's seat. [ ]
2 Franz Kafka was from Berlin. [ ]
3 Kafka's stories were unusual. [ ]
4 The Candangos were from Brasilia. [ ]
5 The Candangos statue is life-size. [ ]
6 "Suzanne Lenglen" is the name of a tennis center. [ ]
7 Lenglen was famous for tennis and for her clothes. [ ]

4 SPEAKING **Do you know any of the people? Do you know any other famous statues? Talk to your partner.**

WRITING
A statue in my town

1 INPUT **Read what Maggie, from Manchester, wrote. Who does she want a statue of and why?**

2 ANALYZE **Read the text again. Find and underline examples of *was/were* and other verbs in the simple past.**

3 **Which parts of the text talk about these things? Write 1, 2, or 3 in the boxes.**

1 why the person/people should have a statue
2 where the writer is from and who the statue is of
3 what the person/people did

4 PLAN **Imagine you can choose to have a statue of a famous person (or famous people) in your town/city. Make notes about these things:**

1 where you live
2 who the person/people is/are
3 what the person/people did
4 why you think they should have a statue

5 PRODUCE **Use your notes from Exercise 3 to write a short text with the title "A Statue in My Town."**

1 Use Maggie's text to help you.
2 Write about 80 words.
3 Check that you used the simple past correctly.

I live in Manchester, in England, and I think it's a good idea to have a statue here of a band called The Stone Roses. [ ]

The band started in 1983 and they only recorded two albums. The first album came out in 1989 and it was a big success. Some people called it "the best British album of all time." They were also famous for their clothes, especially the hat one of the band members liked to wear. The band stopped in 1995, but they played more concerts in 2011 and 2012. They also recorded some new songs in 2015. Then, in 2017, they played their final concerts. [ ]

I think they were important for Manchester because their music helped people all over the world know about the city. [ ]

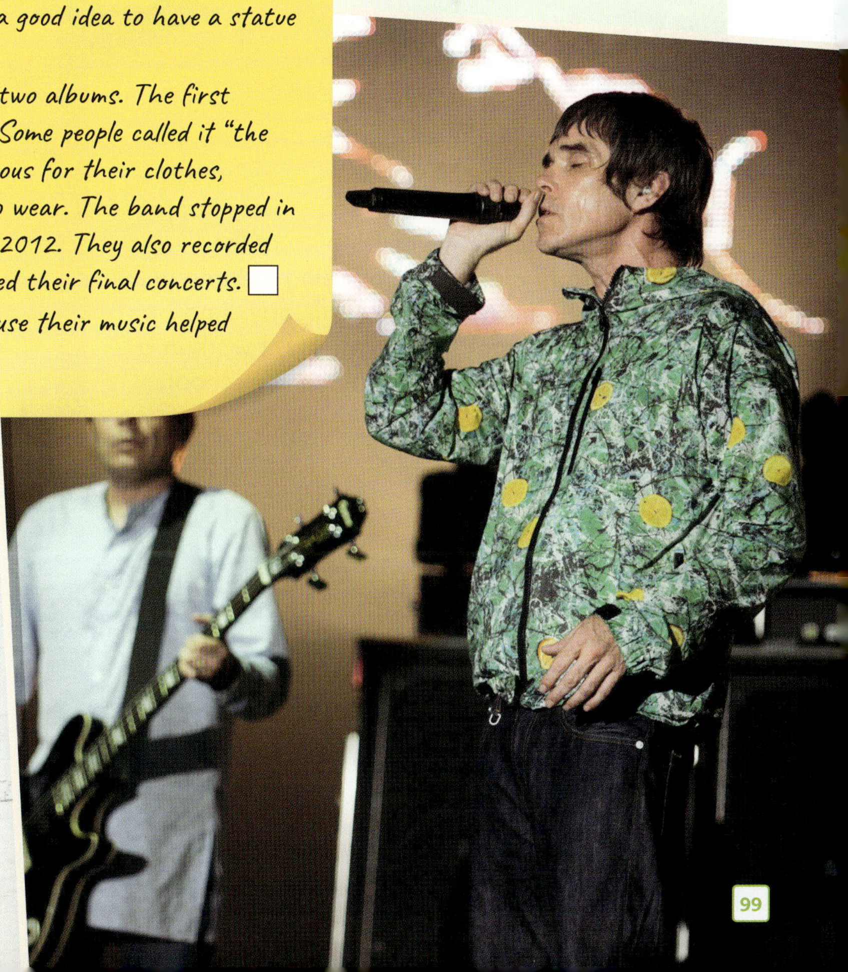

TOWARDS A2 Key for Schools

READING AND WRITING
Multiple matching

1 For these questions, choose the correct answer.

Which person:	James	Maria
1 moved from one country to another?	A	B
2 arrived in London first?	A	B
3 works three days a week?	A	B
4 works and studies?	A	B
5 does not say anything about money?	A	B
6 does not say anything about their dreams for the future?	A	B

I'm from Oxford, but I'm at drama school in London. I arrived here and started school three months ago. It was always my dream to study at drama school, so I'm very happy. It's hard because we need to be at the school from eight in the morning to three in the afternoon, Monday to Thursday. And on Fridays, Saturdays and Sundays, I work in a shop to make money to pay for my school!

I remember arriving in London a year ago, from Spain. It was so exciting. I love it here. I am working for a small IT company. I work six days a week – it's a lot, but for me it's OK. In the future, I want to start my own IT company, and I think this will help me. The people in the company are fun and I'm learning a lot!

LISTENING
3-option multiple choice

2 10.10 **For each question, choose the correct answer.**

1 The new boy is from
A Mexico.
B Spain.
C France.

2 The girl buys
A shoes.
B trousers.
C a coat.

3 The daughter has got
A a headache.
B a sore throat.
C a stomach ache.

4 The son scored
A no goals.
B 3 goals.
C 5 goals.

VOCABULARY

1 Complete the sentences with the words in the list. There are two extra words.

at | carrots | cloudy | in | juice | last | meat | oranges | raining | sandwich | warm | yesterday

1 It's a nice day today. It's ____________ and sunny.
2 Where were you ____________ morning?
3 I love vegetables; ____________ are my favorite.
4 He was born ____________ 2003.
5 They arrived ____________ five thirty.
6 Would you like a chicken and tomato ____________ ?
7 It's very ____________ today. Maybe there'll be rain later.
8 There was a lot of rain ____________ night.
9 Do you want something to drink? Some ____________, perhaps?
10 No chicken or beef, thank you. I don't eat ____________ .

/10

GRAMMAR

2 Complete the sentences with the words in the list.

can | must | mustn't | was | were | would

1 ____________ you like eggs for breakfast?
2 It ____________ a very windy day yesterday.
3 It's her birthday tomorrow. We ____________ remember to say "Happy Birthday."
4 ____________ we watch TV now, please?
5 Meet me at six o'clock, OK? You ____________ be late!
6 There ____________ 200 people at the game on Saturday.

3 Find and correct the mistake in each sentence.

1 Last Sunday morning, we play computer games at home.
2 There was five bananas here yesterday. Where are they?
3 I must to study tonight.
4 Can I having a cheese sandwich, please?
5 I tryed to call you yesterday, but there was no answer.
6 I'm thirsty. I like some water, please.

/12

FUNCTIONAL LANGUAGE

4 Complete the missing words.

1 A Do you want some h _ _ _ with your homework?
B No, t _ _ _ _ _ _, I'm OK.
2 A Where were you y _ _ _ _ _ _ _ _ afternoon?
B I w _ _ at home. Why?
3 A Can you o _ _ _ the window, please?
B Yes, of c _ _ _ _ _ _.
4 B C _ _ I use your phone, please?
B Sure, no p _ _ _ _ _ _.

/8

MY SCORE /30

22–30 😊 10–21 😐 0–9 😣

11 THE ANIMAL WORLD

OBJECTIVES

FUNCTIONS:
asking and answering about past vacations; talking about ability in the past; describing a picture; sequencing (in a story)

GRAMMAR:
simple past: irregular verbs; simple past (negative and questions); *could* / *couldn't*

VOCABULARY:
verb and noun pairs; adjectives

Get THINKING

Watch the video and think: what are your favorite animals?

READING

1 **Match the words in the list with the photos. Write 1–12 in the boxes.**

1 bear | 2 bird | 3 cat | 4 dog | 5 dolphin
6 elephant | 7 gorilla | 8 horse | 9 tiger
10 rabbit | 11 sheep | 12 snake

2 SPEAKING **Complete the sentences with (plural) animals. Use the animals from Exercise 1 or any others that you know. Then compare your ideas with your partner.**

0 Sometimes *snakes* are dangerous.
1 Sometimes you see ____________ in people's houses.
2 You can find ____________ in towns.
3 You can find ____________ in the country.
4 I like ____________ .
5 I don't like ____________ .
6 You can find ____________ on a farm.
7 ____________ can sometimes run very fast.
8 You find ____________ in the ocean.
9 People sometimes eat ____________ .

3 11.01 **Look at the photos on page 103. What do you think the article is about? Read and listen to the article and check your ideas.**

4 **Read the article again. Choose the correct words.**

0 Davide Ceci was with his *mother* / *father*.
1 Davide was *excited* / *scared* in the water.
2 The dolphin found Davide *on top of* / *under* the water.
3 Davide's *brother* / *father* helped him onto the boat.
4 Adam Walker was in the water in *New Zealand* / *Australia*.
5 Adam saw a *whale* / *shark* in the water.
6 A group of *ten* / *twelve* dolphins swam next to Adam.
7 The dolphins stayed with Adam for *60* / *90* minutes.

DOLPHINS TO THE RESCUE

Everyone knows that dolphins are very intelligent animals. But did you know that many scientists believe there is a special connection between dolphins and humans? There are lots of stories about dolphins helping humans who are in danger. Here are two of our favorites.

14-year-old Davide Ceci was in his father's boat off the southeast coast of Italy when he had an accident and fell into the water. Davide didn't know how to swim and his father didn't see him fall, so he didn't stop the boat. He shouted, but his dad didn't hear him. Davide got very worried. Then, without warning, a dolphin came to help him. It gave Davide a push back up to the top of the water and the boy got onto the dolphin's back. The dolphin took him back to the boat. When Davide's father saw his son, he pulled him from the water. The dolphin saved Davide's life!

In 2016, Adam Walker went to New Zealand to swim across the Cook Strait between the North and South Islands. He was swimming when he saw a large dark shape below him. He knew that it was a great white shark and his life was in danger. Adam knew he didn't have a lot of time. A few seconds later, a group of ten dolphins joined him and swam in a circle between him and the shark. The circle of dolphins kept Adam safe. After half an hour, the shark left, but the dolphins swam with him for another hour.

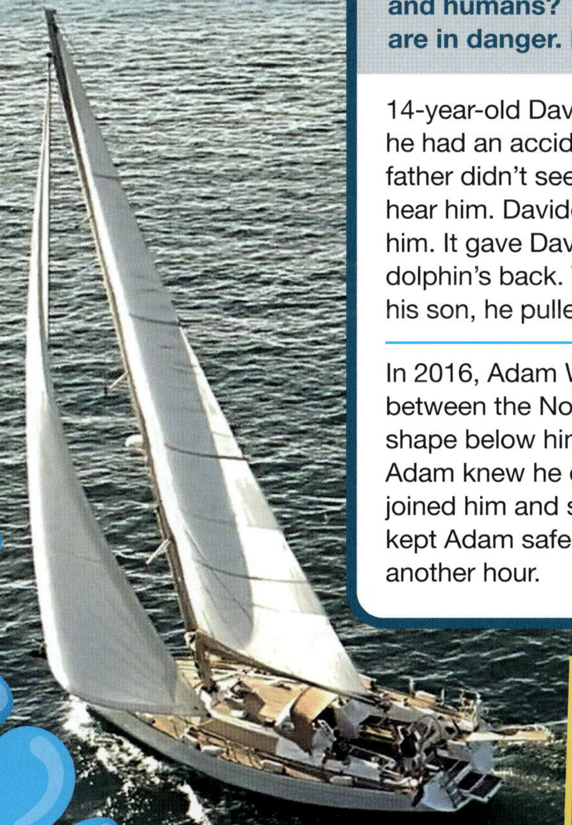

TH!NK values

Animals and us

5 SPEAKING **Dolphins saved the lives of Davide and Adam. Work in pairs. Make a list of things they can do to thank the dolphins.**

6 **Check (✓) the things you agree with.**

- ☐ It's important to be nice to animals.
- ☐ Animals and people can live together.
- ☐ It isn't good to eat animals.
- ☐ It isn't good to use animals for clothes.
- ☐ All animals are important.
- ☐ Zoos are bad for animals.
- ☐ Zoos help people understand animals.
- ☐ It isn't good to have animals in your house.

7 SPEAKING **Work in pairs and compare your ideas from Exercise 6.**

GRAMMAR
Simple past: irregular verbs

1 **Look at these examples from the article on page 103. Find the past tense of the other verbs in article and write them in the table.**

The dolphins **swam** with him for another hour.
After half an hour, the shark **left**.

1	swim	*swam*	7	give	
2	leave	*left*	8	go	
3	come		9	know	
4	fall		10	pull	
5	have		11	see	
6	get		12	take	

2 **Complete the sentences with the simple past form of the words in the list. Use the irregular verbs list on page 128 of the Workbook to help you.**

~~come~~ | drink | eat | fall | forget | get | give | ~~go~~ | run | see | take | write

0 Last weekend, we *went* to Ireland. My grandfather *came* with us.
1 We ____________ some interesting places and ____________ lots of photographs.
2 The boy ____________ too fast and he ____________ over.
3 I ____________ some good presents for my birthday. My parents ____________ me a tablet!
4 I ____________ an email to my teacher, but I ____________ to send it!
5 My friends and I went to a fast food place last night. We ____________ hotdogs and we ____________ orange juice.

Simple past (negative)

3 **These sentences are not true. Use the article on page 103 to correct them. Then choose the correct words to complete the rule.**

0 Davide knew how to swim.
Davide didn't know how to swim.
1 His father saw him fall.
____
2 He stopped the boat.
____

RULE: To make negative sentences in the simple past, we use *didn't* (*did not*) + the [3]*base / past* form of the verb.
It's [4]*the same / different* for both regular and irregular verbs.
It's [5]*the same / different* for all subjects (I/you/they/we/he/she/it).

4 **Make these sentences negative.**

0 I liked the movie. *I didn't like the movie.*
1 I saw my friend at the party. ____________
2 We had a good time. ____________
3 I took a photograph. ____________
4 Our friends came to see us. ____________
5 She found her phone. ____________

→ workbook page 100

VOCABULARY
Verb and noun pairs

5 **Choose the correct words in the sentences from the article on page 103.**

1 Davide *had / did* an accident.
2 Davide *got / did* very worried.
3 Adam knew he should *do / make* something.

6 **Write the phrases in the correct columns. Some of the phrases can go in more than one column.**

~~a break~~ | a good time | a mistake | a noise | a shower | angry | away | excited | homework | on vacation | photos | something

have	take	make
	a break	

do	get	go

7 **Which column(s) do the following words belong in? Can you add more words to the columns?**

a bath | breakfast | fun | a party | skiing | a train

8 **Complete the sentences so they are true for you. Use a positive or negative verb form.**

1 I ____________ breakfast this morning.
2 I ____________ my homework last night.
3 Last weekend, I ____________ a lot of photos with my phone.
4 I ____________ a good time on the weekend.
5 My family ____________ on vacation last year.
6 The last time I went to a party, I ____________ fun.

9 **SPEAKING** **Work in pairs. Compare your answers with a partner.**

→ workbook page 102

LISTENING

10 11.02 **It's the end of the summer break. Mandy meets Josh and asks about his summer. Listen to their conversation. Check (✓) the animals Josh saw and put an ✗ next to the ones he didn't see.**

11 11.02 **Listen again. Complete the sentences with one word.**

1 Josh's family went to the Pantanal in ________________ for the summer.
2 Josh's ________________ really likes birds.
3 One night they heard a jaguar outside their ________________ .
4 It was ________________ when Josh heard the jaguar.
5 Most nights they slept in ________________ .
6 Their guide Sergio spoke ________________ .

SPEAKING

12 Check (✓) the statements that are true for you.

☐ I like camping.
☐ It's exciting to be near animals and nature.
☐ I only want to see animals in a zoo.
☐ I don't like dangerous animals or places.

13 Work in pairs. Talk about the statements in Exercise 12. Do you agree or disagree?

I don't like camping.
Me neither.
I like camping.
Me too.

GRAMMAR
Simple past (questions)

14 Complete the questions from the listening. Write the same word in each space. Then complete the rule.

1 ____________ you have a good vacation?
2 ____________ he speak English?
3 Where ____________ you go?
4 How ____________ you travel around?

RULE: To form the simple past, we use 5____________ + I/you/he/she/it/we/they + the base form of the verb.

15 Put the words in order to make questions.

0 to the party / Did / go / you / ?
Did you go to the party?
1 she / a good time / Did / have / ?
____
2 watch / on TV / Did / that show / you / ?
____
3 they / a lot of / take / photos / Did / ?
____
4 What / for breakfast / did / have / you / ?
____
5 did / you / Where / last night / go / ?
____

16 Complete the dialogues.

0 A What *did you watch* last night?
B I watched a really good movie.
1 A Where ________________ on Saturday?
B I went to the movies.
2 A What ________________ at the zoo?
B We saw some really cool animals!
3 A What ________________ in Italy?
B We ate spaghetti and lasagna.

17 SPEAKING **Work in pairs. Write questions to ask your partner about their last vacation. Then ask and answer.**

... go? *... stay?* *... do?* *... a good time?* *... photos?* *... on your own?*

→ workbook page 101

PRONUNCIATION
Simple past irregular verbs Go to page 121.

READING

1 Look at the pictures. These animals don't exist today: they are extinct. Match them with the names in the article. Write 1–3 in the boxes.

2 11.05 Read and listen to the article. Check your answers.

EXTINCT ANIMALS

A ☐

B ☐

C ☐

1 THE GREAT AUK

The great auk was a large seabird that lived in the North Atlantic. It was a bird, but it couldn't fly. It could swim underwater really well. It caught and ate fish when it dived under the water. Its feathers were very soft and people used them to make pillows for their beds. Because of this, people killed the birds. The last great auk died on the island of Eldey in 1835.

2 THE TASMANIAN TIGER

The Tasmanian tiger was only found in Australia, Tasmania, and New Guinea. It got its name because it had stripes like a tiger, but it was not a member of the cat family. Farmers believed Tasmanian tigers killed their sheep, so they paid people to kill them. Many of the tigers died after getting sick from diseases they caught from other animals. The last Tasmanian tiger died in Hobart Zoo in 1936.

3 STELLER'S SEA COW

Steller's sea cow was a large animal that lived in the cold Arctic waters around Alaska. It grew up to nine meters long. Because it was so big, it couldn't go under the water. It ate the plants on top of the water. It wasn't a very dangerous animal – it was quite friendly. Because of this, it was very easy to kill. Europeans first found the sea cow in 1741. 27 years later, they killed the last one.

3 Read the article again. Write the names of the animals.

0 This animal was a bird, but it couldn't fly. *great auk*

1 This animal was the last to go. ________

2 Farmers didn't like this animal. ________

3 This animal lived in the ocean, but couldn't go underwater. ________

4 People killed this bird for its feathers. ________

5 This animal was not afraid of humans. ________

4 SPEAKING Do you know any other animals that are extinct? Talk to your partner.

GRAMMAR
could / couldn't (ability)

5 Complete the examples from the article on page 106. Then read the rule.

1 It ___________ swim under water really well.
2 It was so big, it ___________ go under the water.

> **RULE:** We use *could / couldn't* + the base form of a verb to talk about ability in the past.

6 Use *could/couldn't* and a verb from the list to complete the sentences.

~~do~~ | drive | play | ride | see | speak

0 The homework last night was very difficult. *I couldn't do* it! ✗
1 My grandmother ___________ without her glasses. ✗
2 My brother ___________ the guitar when he was only seven. ✓
3 I ___________ a bicycle when I was four. ✓
4 My dad ___________ a car until he was 25. ✗
5 My grandfather was amazing; he ___________ five languages. ✓

7 SPEAKING Work in pairs. Think about what you could or couldn't do when you were five. Use the ideas in the list. Add your own ideas.

cook	speak English
dance	swim
read and write	take photos
ride a bicycle	use a tablet

When I was five, I couldn't ride a bicycle.

When I was five, I could swim.

→ workbook page 101

VOCABULARY
Adjectives

8 11.06 Write the words in the list under the photos. There are six extra words you don't need. Listen and check.

beautiful | boring | clean | dangerous | dirty | horrible
interesting | lovely | safe | smart | stupid | ugly

1 ___________

4 ___________

2 ___________

5 ___________

3 ___________

6 ___________

9 SPEAKING Work in pairs or in small groups. Use the adjectives from Exercise 8 to talk about these things.

a famous person | a sport you like | a TV show | your town

I think our town is ugly.

Really? I think it's beautiful.

10 Match the adjectives and their opposites from Exercise 8.

→ workbook page 102

WRITING
An extinct animal

11 Choose an animal that is extinct. Try to find the answers to these questions.

1 What kind of animal was it?
2 Where did it live?
3 What did it look like?
4 What could it do/not do?
5 Why did it die out?

12 SPEAKING Work in pairs. Tell your partner about your animal.

13 Use your answers from Exercise 11 to write a short text (60–90 words) about the animal.

DEVELOPING SPEAKING

1 **Look at the photo. Where is the boy?**

2 11.07 **Now read and listen to the dialogue. Who's afraid of snakes?**

Lena: Hey, Nathan. How are you? Did you have a good weekend?
Nathan: Well, sort of. I mean ... it was OK.
Lena: You don't sound very sure! What happened?
Toby: Yeah, come on, tell us.
Nathan: All right. Well, on Sundays we usually go for a walk, my family and I. But yesterday, I went alone.
Toby: Where did you go?
Nathan: I went to the forest – you know, outside town. It's really nice there. And I started walking, when suddenly ...
Lena: Yes? Suddenly what?
Nathan: Well, in front of me, there was a snake.
Toby: Are there snakes in the forest? Are you sure?
Nathan: Yes, I'm sure. It was on the path. I stopped. I didn't do anything. Then it just went away. I was afraid.
Lena: Poor you! I hate snakes, too.
Toby: Why were you afraid? It's just a snake. A snake can't kill you.
Lena: Some snakes can! Anyway, it's OK to be afraid sometimes.
Nathan: Thanks, Lena. Anyway, that's why my weekend was just OK.

3 SPEAKING **Read the dialogue again. Answer the questions with a partner.**
1 What was different about Nathan's walk this Sunday?
2 What did he see in front of him?
3 What did he do?
4 Who thinks it was OK for Nathan to be afraid?

Phrases for fluency

4 **Find the expressions 1–4 in the dialogue. Who says them? How do you say them in your language?**
1 What happened? ________
2 All right. ________
3 suddenly ... ________
4 Poor you! ________

5 **Put the sentences in the correct order to make a dialogue.**
- [ ] **Gio** It's true. I was so afraid I jumped on the chair and fell off!
- [ ] **Gio** Because I saw a big, horrible spider!
- [1] **Gio** Can I tell you what happened yesterday?
- [ ] **Gio** I was in the kitchen, and suddenly, I fell off my chair.
- [ ] **Natalie** What? You saw a spider and fell off your chair?
- [ ] **Natalie** All right. What happened?
- [ ] **Natalie** Oh, poor you! But why?

6 **Complete the dialogues with the expressions from Exercise 4.**
0 A You look really happy! *What happened?*
B I got my test results. 95%!
1 A I think I'm sick.
B ______________ ! Maybe you should stay in bed today.
2 A Dad was horrible last night.
B I know. At first he was OK, but ______________ he got angry!
3 A There's a great new online computer game. Can I play it, Dad?
B ______________ , but only for half an hour. You have homework.

FUNCTIONS
Sequencing (in a story)

KEY LANGUAGE
First, ...
Then, ...
After that, ...
Later, ...
Finally, ... / In the end, ...

7 **What did Jake do yesterday? Choose the correct word for every sentence.**
[1]*After that, / First,* Jake got up and took a shower. [2]*Then, / In the end,* he had breakfast and did his homework. [3]*After that, / Finally,* he went to his grandma's house for lunch. [4]*In the end, / Later,* he went to the movies with his friend Bruno. [5]*Finally, / First,* he went to bed.

8 **Think of a story to tell a partner. Use one of the ideas below or your own idea. Make notes.**
- what you did last weekend
- what you did on your last birthday
- something funny that happened to you

9 SPEAKING **Tell your partner your story. Use the sequencing words from the Key Language box to structure your story.**

LIFE COMPETENCIES

Everyone is scared of something – a person, a thing, or a situation at some time in their life. By being positive and trying new things, we can face our fear and even beat it!

1 ▶33 **Watch the vlog. Check (✓) the things Ethan is scared of.**

2 ▶33 **Watch the vlog again. What advice can you give Ethan?**

3 Read the dialogues. What are Tom, Nadia, and Lara afraid of?

1 **Harry** Come on, I don't want to walk up the stairs to the fifth floor.
Tom Sorry, no. I can't get into an elevator, no way.
Harry Why? Did something happen to you?
Tom Yes. When I was only six, I got stuck in an elevator for 20 minutes! It was awful. I was so scared.
Harry Oh, poor you. But look, it's only five floors and it's only you and me here. I can help you and talk to you.
Tom OK. Yes, I'll try. Here's the elevator now. Let's go in.

2 **Nadia** Look, there's that boy, Alex. He's so nice.
Sadie Yes, he's a nice guy – and I know you like him. So, go and say hello. Talk to him.
Nadia No, I can't do that! I'm too scared.
Sadie Scared of what? You're nice, too – I'm sure he likes you.
Nadia But …
Sadie No buts. Come on, let's go and say hi.

3 **Lara** This is great. I love running! Oh, wait! Oh, no!
Grace What's the matter, Lara? Are you tired?
Lara No, that's not it. Look, there's a dog over there. I'm scared.
Grace Of that little dog? It can't hurt you! It's asleep. And it's really small, too.
Lara But I'm really scared of dogs, Grace. Can we turn around and run back now, please?
Grace Oh, Lara, don't be silly! Come on.

4 SPEAKING **Ask and answer the questions with a partner.**

1 Why is Tom scared of elevators?
2 How does Harry help Tom?
3 Why do you think Nadia is scared of talking to Alex?
4 What does Grace say that isn't supportive?

Me and my world

5 Make a list of things that people are often scared of.

6 SPEAKING **Work in pairs. Are you scared of any of the things on your lists? What can people do to not be afraid?**

TIPS FOR FACING OUR FEARS

- Remember that everybody is afraid of something.
- Remember that it is often possible to stop feeling afraid of something.
- You shouldn't stop doing the things you want to do.

12 MOVING AROUND

OBJECTIVES

FUNCTIONS:
talking about travel and transportation; comparing things; at the train station

GRAMMAR:
comparative adjectives; *one* / *ones*

VOCABULARY:
transportation; geographical places

Get THINKING

Watch the video and think: what forms of transportation do you use?

A ☐

B ☐

C ☐

D ☐

E ☐

READING

1 **Match the words in the list with the photos. Write 1–5 in the boxes.**

1 a bike | **2** a boat | **3** a bus | **4** a car | **5** a subway train

2 SPEAKING **Work in pairs. When do you use the forms of transportation in Exercise 1?**

I go to my friend's house by bike.

I go to school by bus.

3 **Put the forms of transportation in Exercise 1 in order of speed: 1 = slow, 5 = fast.**

4 12.01 **Read and listen to the article and write the type of transportation under each medal.**

1 ________ 2 ________ 3 ________ 4 ________

5 **Read the article again and match the questions with the answers.**

0 Why did the TV show hosts have a race? *d*
1 Why did they choose different types of transportation? ☐
2 Why was there a surprise? ☐
3 Why weren't the hosts happy? ☐
4 What did the hosts say about the bike? ☐
5 Why is the bike good to use in a city? ☐

a To find the best one.
b Because they wanted the car to win.
c Because it is cheap, clean, and healthy.
d To find the best way to get across Manhattan.
e It was dangerous.
f Because the bike won.

A lot of big cities, like New York, have many traffic problems. Sometimes a trip of a few kilometers can take more than an hour. So what's the best way to get across Manhattan? For a very short trip, it's probably a good idea to walk. But what happens when you want to go farther?

The hosts of a popular TV show about cars decided to find out. Each of the hosts chose a different type of transportation to make the same trip. One host went by bike. One went by car. Another chose public transportation – the subway and bus – and the last one traveled by speedboat up the Hudson River. They all started at the same time and the same place in Battery Park, but who got to the Upper West Side first?

The results were a surprise. The bike came in first. In second place was the speedboat. Public transportation came in third and the car was last.

So the hosts had an answer. The bike was faster than all the other types of transportation and the car was slower. They weren't very happy with the result because they wanted the car to win. They made a joke and said the bike wasn't a real winner because it was more dangerous.

But, of course, the bike is the real winner. It's the best way to move around. It's cheaper than public transportation and it is healthier than going by car. It's also better for our cities because bikes don't make the air dirty. So next time you need to travel around, think before you and your parents get into the car – "Can we make this trip by bike?"

THINK values

Transportation and the environment

6 **Choose the title that best sums up the article.**

a Cars are great ☐
b The great race ☐
c Get on your bike ☐
d Be careful on your bike ☐

7 SPEAKING **Tell your partner what title you chose and why.**

8 **How friendly to the environment do you think these types of transportation are? Write 1–6 in the boxes: 1 = best, 6 = worst.**

☐ bus ☐ car ☐ plane
☐ bike ☐ motorcycle ☐ train

9 SPEAKING **Work in pairs and compare your answers.**

VOCABULARY
Transportation

1 12.02 **Match the words in the list with the photos. Write 1–6 in the boxes. Listen and check.**

1 ferry | 2 helicopter | 3 motorcycle
4 ~~plane~~ | 5 taxi | 6 train

2 **Look at the photos in Exercise 1 and answer the questions.**

Which types of transportation travel …

1 on roads? ______________

3 on water? ______________

2 on rails? ______________

4 in the air? ______________

3 SPEAKING **Can you add any other types of transportation to the lists?**

→ workbook page 110

Grammar rap!

GRAMMAR
Comparative adjectives

4 **Look at the article on page 111. Check (✓) the sentence that isn't true. Then complete the table and the rule.**

1 Bikes are *cheaper than* public transportation. ☐
2 Going by bike is *healthier than* going by car. ☐
3 Cars are *more dangerous than* bikes. ☐
4 Bikes are *better than* other types of transportation. ☐

adjective	comparative	
fast	faster	
big	bigger	
cheap	5 ______________	
easy	easier	+ than
healthy	6 ______________	
expensive	more expensive	
dangerous	7 ______________	
good	8 ______________	

RULE: Short adjectives: We usually add *-er*. If the adjective ends in consonant + *-y*, change the *y* to 9 ______________, e.g., *easy* – ***easier***. If the adjective ends in vowel + consonant, double the consonant, e.g., *big* – ***bigger***.
Long adjectives: We add the word 10 ______________ before the adjective.
Irregular adjectives: We use a different word, e.g., *good* – *better*, *bad* – 11 ______________ .
After comparative adjectives we use ***than***.

5 **Write the comparative form of these adjectives.**

1 exciting	2 slow	3 difficult
4 happy	5 safe	6 small
7 funny	8 hot	9 fast

6 **Look at the types of transportation on this page. Write four sentences to compare them.**

7 SPEAKING **Work in pairs. Read your sentences to your partner, but don't say one of the forms of transportation. Your partner guesses what it is.**

They are faster than buses.

Cars!

→ workbook page 108

PRONUNCIATION
Word stress – comparatives Go to page 121.

LISTENING

8 12.05 **Kate wants to travel to Boston. She's at the train station. Listen to the conversation and complete the details of her trip.**

Providence, Rhode Island (leave)	1 ________
Boston, Massachusetts (arrive)	12:46 p.m.

Price
- one-way: $16.00
- round-trip: 2 ________
- flexible: 3 ________

Platform
- Departs: 4 ________
- Arrives: 1 pm

9 12.05 **Listen again. Answer the questions.**

1 Why doesn't Kate want to take the earlier train to Boston?
2 When does Kate want to return to Providence?
3 Who does Kate want to meet in Boston?
4 How many platforms are at Back Bay station?

FUNCTIONS
At the train station

10 Look at these sentences. Who says them? Write SA (sales assistant) or C (customer) in the boxes.

0 Good morning. How can I help you? SA
1 What time's the next train? ☐
2 What time does that one arrive in Boston? ☐
3 Do you want a one-way ticket or a round-trip ticket? ☐
4 How often are the trains to Boston? ☐
5 OK, that's $32.00, please. ☐
6 What platform does the train leave from? ☐
7 Have a good trip. ☐

11 SPEAKING **Work in pairs. Use this information and prepare a similar dialogue. Act out your dialogue.**

________ (leave)	11 a.m.	11:15 a.m.
________ (arrive)	11:45 a.m.	12 p.m.

Price
- one-way: $12.00
- round trip: $20.00

platform
- Departs: 2
- Arrives: 3

Train to THINK
Comparing

12 Write the words in the list in the correct place in the diagram.

cheap | dangerous | drive | engine | fast
healthy | lights | radio | ride | wheels

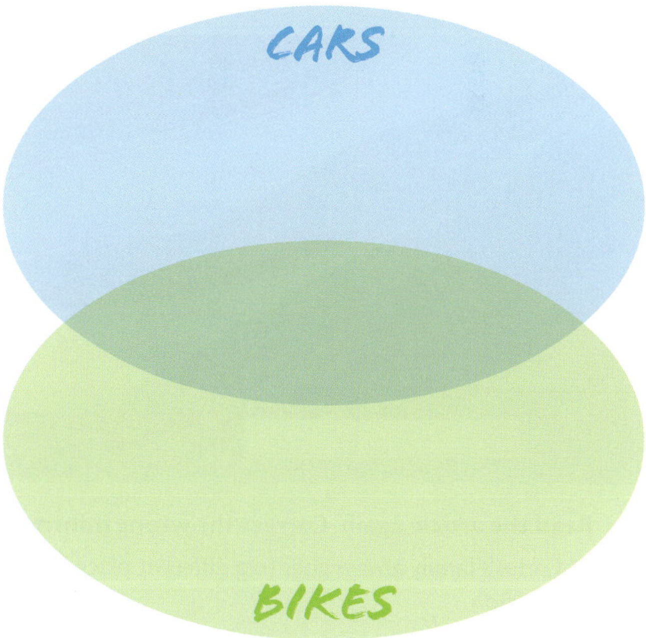

13 Think of more words to add to the diagram.

14 SPEAKING **Work in pairs. Compare the two forms of transportation. Use comparative adjectives.**

In Boston, bikes are faster than cars.

READING

1 12.06 **Read and listen to the magazine article. Write the names under the photos.**

Carlos | Julia | Miriam | Nathan

MY FAVORITE TRIP

We all love going on trips. Here are some of your favorites. Thank you for sharing them!

Carlos *Posted 5 minutes ago*

Every year my family goes on vacation to a small town by the ocean. It has really beautiful beaches and we always have a great time. I love the trip there. We always go by train. It takes about four hours, but I don't mind. I'm always so excited. I just love watching the mountains and forests go by.

Julia *Posted 10 minutes ago*

What's my favorite trip? Any one with my mom on her motorcycle. I don't care where we go, I just love being on her bike. She's a really good rider and I always feel safe. I love the wind on my face as we ride through the countryside.

Miriam *Posted 40 minutes ago*

My favorite trip is my walk to school. We live on a farm, and my school is about one kilometer away. Every morning, I walk across the fields and then I go along the river until I'm at school. It's a really beautiful walk. I love looking for birds. There are some lovely ones. And sometimes if I'm lucky, I see a rabbit. I love my walk to school … but I love the walk home more!

Nathan *Posted 50 minutes ago*

My grandparents live in Miami. We visit them every year and, of course, we go by plane. It's a three-hour trip, but I love it. I love traveling by plane. It's so exciting. I never get bored because there are a lot of movies to watch. They always have really good ones.

A ____________

B ____________

C ____________

D ____________

2 **Read the article again. Correct the wrong information in these sentences.**

0 Carlos's family always goes to a different place on vacation.
the same ____________

1 His train trip takes six hours.
____

2 Julia loves riding on her dad's motorcycle.
____

3 Miriam likes her walk to the local store.
____

4 She likes the walk to school more than the walk home.
____

5 Nathan's cousins live in Miami.
____

3 SPEAKING **Work in pairs. Talk about your trip to and from school.**

GRAMMAR
one / ones

4 Look at the examples from the article on page 114. What do the words *one* and *ones* refer to? Then complete the rule with *plural* and *singular*.

1 What's my favorite trip? Any one with my mom on her motorcycle.

2 I never get bored because there are a lot of movies to watch. They always have really good ones.

> **RULE:** To avoid repeating a noun, we often use *one* in place of [3]__________ nouns and *ones* in place of [4]__________ nouns.

5 Write *one* or *ones* in the spaces to replace the crossed out words.

0 **A** Do you want to watch this movie?
B No, I've seen that ~~movie~~ ___*one*___ before.

1 **A** Do you want to try on these jeans?
B No, I'd like to try on the ~~jeans~~ __________ behind them.

2 **A** What bus can we take?
B Any ~~bus~~ __________ that has "Downtown" on the front of it.

3 I have three children. The oldest ~~child~~ __________ is a boy and the younger ~~children~~ __________ are girls.

4 There's a bank on Main Street and there's another ~~bank~~ __________ on Market Street.

5 I have lots of books, but my favorite ~~books~~ __________ are my bird books.

→ workbook page 109

VOCABULARY
Geographical places

6 Complete the words with the first and last letters. Use the article on page 114 to help you.

0 m *o u n t a i* n

1 _ e a c _

2 _ i v e _

3 _ c e _ n

4 _ i e l _

5 _ a k _

6 _ a r _

7 _ o r e s _

7 SPEAKING Work in pairs. Make a list of famous …

a beaches
b rivers
c oceans
d lakes

8 Think about your favorite trip. Make notes.

Where to	
How	
Who with	

9 SPEAKING Tell your partner about your trip.

My favorite trip is to the mountains to go skiing.

How do you get there?

We go by car.

→ workbook page 110

THINK
Transportation around the world

Culture

TRANSPORTATION AROUND THE WORLD

1 ______________

3 ______________

2 ______________

4 ______________

THE AMFIBUS, THE NETHERLANDS

The big, blue Amfibus certainly makes a big splash! It's in Rotterdam and it takes people on tours of the city. It's cool. It can travel on land and in the water. It is more expensive than water taxis, but it is more exciting, too. It is slower in the water than on land. It goes at 8 kmph in the water and 96 kmph on land. The tour lasts for an hour and it costs 27.50 euros.

THE URBAN CABLE CAR, TURKEY

Ankara's cable car is cheaper than other forms of public transportation and it is healthier because it doesn't pollute the air. It is also easier and faster than traveling by car because there are no traffic jams in the sky! It travels 60 meters above the ground and passengers can get great views of the city.

MOVING WALKWAYS AND ESCALATORS, HONG KONG

The Central-Mid-Levels Escalator is 800 meters long. Escalators are usually inside a shopping mall or an airport, but not this one! It's outside. It's a great way to travel around this city of hills. And it's free! There are 14 places where you can get on and off. The escalators travel down the hill from 6 a.m. to 10 a.m. so people can travel to work. They travel up the hill from 10 a.m. to midnight.

SUBMARINES, LANZAROTE AND TENERIFE

Now you can travel in a submarine! This submarine carries tourists. It is a safe and comfortable way to see the colorful fish and the plants and rocks in the ocean. The submarine can carry 48 people and it has 11 large windows on each side. It travels down 60 meters under the water.

1 **Look at the photos on page 116. Find these things.**

a bus | a cable car | a city | an escalator | a submarine | water

2 12.07 **Read and listen to the article. Write the name of the form of transportation under the photos.**

3 **Read the article again and check (✓) the correct boxes.**

	the Amfibus	urban cable car	escalator	submarine
1 You have a great view of the city.	☐	☐	☐	☐
2 You often see these in a shopping mall or an airport.	☐	☐	☐	☐
3 It travels on water and on land.	☐	☐	☐	☐
4 It is a faster way to travel than by car.	☐	☐	☐	☐
5 It's a safe and comfortable way to travel underwater.	☐	☐	☐	☐

4 SPEAKING **Discuss these questions with a partner.**

1 Which of these types of transportation would you most like to travel on?
2 Are there any unusual types of transportation in your country? Where?

WRITING
Unusual forms of transportation

1 INPUT **Read the text. What's the name of the form of transportation?**

2 ANALYZE **Read the text again and answer the questions.**

1 Where can you see it?
2 What type of transportation is it?
3 Why is it unusual?

3 PLAN **Choose one of these unusual forms of transportation or one that you already know about. Look on the Internet for information. Make notes to answer the questions in Exercise 2.**

The Chiva bus, Colombia
The Coco Taxi, Cuba
The Hovercraft, Isle of Wight, UK

4 PRODUCE **Use your notes to write a short text about your form of transportation from Exercise 3. Write 60–100 words.**

THE ICE ANGEL IN WISCONSIN

Wisconsin is a state in the US. There are large lakes in Wisconsin. One of the lakes is named Lake Superior. In the winter, it is very cold and the water in the lake turns to ice. When the ice is hard, cars can drive across it. But sometimes the ice is very thin. Then, only the Ice Angel can cross it. The Ice Angel is a very special bus. It can travel on water, snow, and ice. In the summer, it travels on water and in the winter, it travels across the ice. It takes people from Wisconsin's Madeline Island to Bayfield.

TOWARDS A2 Key for Schools

READING AND WRITING
Short message

1 **You want to go out and have lunch with your English friend Reese on Sunday. Write an email to Reese.**

In the email:

- ask Reese to go out for lunch with you on Sunday
- say where you would like to go for lunch
- say what you would like to eat.

Write 25 words or more.

Part 7: Picture story

2 **Look at the three pictures. Write the story shown in the pictures. Write 35 words or more.**

LISTENING
3-option multiple choice

3 12.08 **Listen to Polly talking to her friend Seth about their pets. For each question choose the right answer (A, B or C).**

1 Spot is
 A Polly's dog. B Seth's dog. C Seth's mum's dog.
2 Flopsie is a
 A rabbit. B cat. C dog.
3 Polly's pet is a
 A rabbit called Nemo. B fish called Nemo. C cat called Nemo.
4 Nemo eats once a
 A day. B week. C month.
5 Polly cleans Nemo's bowl
 A every week. B three times a week. C once a month.

TEST YOURSELF UNITS 11 & 12

VOCABULARY

1 Complete the sentences with the words in the list. There are two extra words.

did | do | farm | forest | fun | get | go | had | horrible | motorcycle | safe | taxi

1 That river is dirty and ugly. I think it's ______________________ .
2 Let's have some ______________________ this weekend. How about going to the beach?
3 We went to the beach last weekend and we ______________________ a really good time.
4 There are lots of animals on that ______________________ .
5 It's snowing! Let's ______________________ skiing this afternoon.
6 Dangerous? No, it's very ______________________ , I promise.
7 The weekend was really boring. I just ______________________ my homework, nothing else.
8 I don't think it's a good idea to ride a ______________________ in a big city.
9 It's not a big deal. Please don't ______________________ angry about it.
10 We missed the last bus so we took a ______________________ to get home.

/10

GRAMMAR

2 Complete the sentences with the words in the list.

better | couldn't | did | good | more | ones | went

1 I was sick, so I ______________________ go to your party, sorry.
2 Green? No thanks, I like the blue ______________________ over there.
3 I love that movie. It's really ______________________ .
4 ______________________ you have fun at the party?
5 My new phone was ______________________ expensive than my old one.
6 This song is ______________________ than the last one.
7 I couldn't go to the concert, but my friends ______________________ .

3 Find and correct the mistake in each sentence.

1 Are these your new shoes or are they the old one?
2 My parents gived me this book for my birthday.
3 The chicken was horrible so I not eat it.
4 Went you to the beach last weekend?
5 I like these jeans because they're cheaper as the other ones.
6 I'm bad at physics, but Jack is more bad!
7 Did you saw any good movies last week?

/14

FUNCTIONAL LANGUAGE

4 Complete the missing words.

1 A Hi. Can I have a t _ _ _ _ _ to New York, please?
B OK. O _ _ w _ _ or r _ _ _ _ _ t _ _ _?
2 A What time is the n _ _ _ train to Boston, please?
B 3:00 – and after that, there's a train at 3:45.
A OK. I want the 3:00 train. What platform does it l _ _ _ _ from?
B Platform 4. Have a good t _ _ _!

/6

MY SCORE /30

22–30 | 10–21 | 0–9

PRONUNCIATION

UNIT 7
Vowel sound /ɔr/

1 7.02 **Read and listen to the dialogue.**

Paul Do you like **sports**?
Laura Oh, yes, it's very **important**. I love **skateboarding**.
Paul So do I! Are there any **more sports** you like?
Laura Well, I like all ball games. Hmm … what time is it, Paul?
Paul It's a **quarter** to **four**, **Laura**.
Laura I have to go. I'm playing soccer at **four**.

2 **Say the words in blue. Which vowel sound do they all have?**

3 7.03 **Listen again and repeat. Then practice with a partner.**

UNIT 8
Intonation – listing items

1 8.05 **Read and listen to the dialogue.**

Mom I'm going shopping. Do you want anything?
Brad Yes, Mom! I need a T-shirt. Oh, and some socks, please.
Mom OK. A T-shirt and socks …
Brad Actually, I need a T-shirt, socks, sneakers, a jacket, and a baseball cap.
Mom A T-shirt, socks, sneakers, a jacket, and a baseball cap. I think you need to come with me!

2 **Brad wants *a T-shirt, socks, sneakers, a jacket,* and *a baseball cap*. Circle the arrows to show when his voice goes up and when it goes down.**

3 8.06 **Listen again and repeat. Then practice with a partner.**

UNIT 9
Intonation – giving two choices

1 9.06 **Read and listen to the dialogue.**

Server Would you like salad or soup?
Mike Salad, please.
Server Chicken or fish?
Mike I think I'll have fish today.
Server Would you like dessert?
Mike Yes, please!
Server Cake or fruit?
Mike Hmm … I'll have the fruit.
Server And coffee or tea?
Mike Oh, coffee, please.

2 9.07 **Circle the arrows in the dialogue to show when the server's voice goes up and when it goes down. Listen and check.**

3 9.07 **Listen again and repeat. Then practice with a partner.**

UNIT 10
Simple past regular verbs

1 10.06 **Read and listen to the story.**

My grandmother **lived** in the country. She **walked** to town to go to school. She **started** working in a bottle factory. She **worked** in the factory until she **married** my grandfather. One day, she **invented** a machine that cleaned bottles. The factory **wanted** the machine and my grandparents were rich after that!

2 **The *-ed* ending is pronounced differently in the red and blue words. What's the difference?**

3 10.07 **Listen again and repeat. Then practice with a partner.**

UNIT 11
Simple past irregular verbs

1 11.03 **Read and listen to the dialogue.**

Peter	**Could** you ride a bike when you were young, Grandma?
Grandma	I certainly **could**, Peter. I **went** to school on my bike. I **put** my books in the basket.
Peter	**Could** you swim?
Grandma	Of course I **could**! One day I **swam** across the lake near my house.

2 **Say the past tense words in blue. What is the base form of these verbs?**

3 11.04 **Listen again and repeat. Then practice with a partner.**

UNIT 12
Word stress – comparatives

1 12.03 **Read and listen to the sentences.**

A plane is faster than a car.
A bike is slower than a train.
A speedboat is quicker than a ferry.

2 **Find the comparative adjective in each sentence. Which syllable is stressed in each of these words?**

3 12.04 **Listen again and repeat. Then practice with a partner.**

GET IT RIGHT!

UNIT 7

can / can't

Learners sometimes use the wrong form of the verb when they use *can* and *to*.

We use the infinitive without *to* after *can*.

✓ *He can play the piano.*

✗ *He ~~can to play~~ the piano.*

We use *to* + infinitive after *want* and *need*.

✓ *They want to know the answer.*

✗ *They ~~want know~~ the answer.*

Correct the mistakes in the sentences.

0 He needs do that.
He needs to do that.
1 Can you to speak Spanish?
2 We want do some shopping.
3 You need clean your room.
4 I need eat something. I'm hungry!
5 I can't to do my homework.
6 Alex wants do everything.

UNIT 8

like / don't like + verb + *-ing*

Learners sometimes use the wrong form of the verb where *-ing* is required.

We use the *-ing* form of verbs after the verbs *like, don't like, love,* and *hate*.

✓ *I like playing tennis.*

✗ *I ~~like play~~ tennis.*

✗ *I ~~like to playing~~ tennis.*

Correct the mistakes in the sentences.

0 I like read books.
I like reading books.
1 I like sing and dancing.
2 We love go shopping.
3 She likes to wearing green clothes.
4 They don't like play basketball.
5 Paul doesn't hate study.
6 Anna likes to wearing white clothes.

UNIT 9

must / mustn't / can / would

Learners often have trouble spelling modal verbs *can't, must, would,* and *mustn't*.

Correct the spelling mistakes in the sentences.

0 Wold you like to go with me?
Would you like to go with me?
1 I cant find the coffee.
2 You mast learn English.
3 I woud like to do some shopping.
4 You musn't use YouTube©.
5 Woudn't you like some more?
6 We mussn't be late.

UNIT 10

was / wasn't, were / weren't

Learners sometimes confuse *was* and *were*.

***Was, wasn't, were,* and *weren't* all have to agree with the subject.**

✓ *The jeans were very beautiful.*

✗ *The jeans ~~was~~ very beautiful.*

Check (✓) the correct sentences and put an ✗ next to the incorrect ones. Correct the mistakes.

0 There was a lot of people. [✗]
There were a lot of people.
1 We was at Dan's house all night. [ ]
2 There was a lot of food. [ ]
3 Wasn't you there? [ ]
4 I were happy to see you on the weekend. [ ]
5 How many people were at your house? [ ]
6 Last night there were a party on the beach. [ ]
7 He was my friend at school. [ ]
8 Katie and Jo was there. [ ]

UNIT 11

Simple past (irregular verbs)

Learners sometimes use the wrong forms of irregular verbs in the simple past or misspell them.

✓ *I paid a lot of money.*

✗ *I ~~payed~~ a lot of money.*

Correct the mistakes in the sentences.

0 I haved a vacation.
I had a vacation.
1 I maked a lot of friends.
2 She gived me a lot of presents.
3 Jack and Al taked photographs.
4 There where some problems with his work.
5 I cam home late yesterday.
6 He swimmed very fast.
7 They goed to the movies.
8 Helen mad some food.

Simple past (negative)

Learners sometimes use the simple present negative where the simple past is required.

✓ *I didn't find the answer before the end of the exam.*

✗ *I ~~don't~~ find the answer before the end of the exam.*

Choose the correct options.

0 We *don't* / *didn't* go to the game last week.
1 I *didn't* / *don't* need any help at the moment.
2 I bought some T-shirts, but I *didn't* / *don't* buy any tops.
3 I went to a store, but I *didn't* / *don't* like the phones there.
4 Do you like chicken? No, I *didn't* / *don't* eat meat.
5 I had a lot of presents, but he *didn't* / *don't* give me one.
6 We *didn't* / *don't* usually go on vacation because we like being at home.

UNIT 12

Comparative adjectives

Learners often use *more* and *-er* in the same sentence when only one of these forms is required.
We form comparative adjectives by adding *-er* if the adjective has one syllable (or two syllables ending in *-y*) and by using *more* if the adjective has two or more syllables. We don't use *more* and *-er* together.

✓ *This one is bigger than that one.*

✗ *This one is ~~more bigger~~ than that one.*

✗ *This one is ~~more big~~ than that one.*

Correct the mistakes in the sentences.

0 The train is more cheap than the plane.
The train is cheaper than the plane.
1 He is more healthier than he was last year.
2 Henry is more older than his brother.
3 My cell phone is more newer than my brother's.
4 Basketball is more good than baseball.
5 I was more happy than Joe at the end of the game.
6 Henry's brother is more friendlier than Henry.
7 I think math is more easy than English.

than with comparative adjectives

Learners sometimes use *then* or *that* where *than* is required with comparative adjectives.

✓ *Colin is older than Oliver.*

✗ *Colin is older ~~then~~ Oliver.*

✗ *Colin is older ~~that~~ Oliver.*

Complete the sentences with *then*, *that*, or *than*.

0 He can run faster ___*than*___ me.
1 It is much better ____________ your cell phone.
2 Call me ____________ .
3 It is more ____________ I thought.
4 ____________ is my book.
5 This one is better than ____________ one.
6 We danced and ____________ watched a movie.

STUDENT A

UNIT 8, PAGE 79, TRAIN TO THINK

Student A

Listen to the questions your partner asks about the picture in Exercise 2. Answer with short answers. Correct the negative answers.

1 Are there ten people in the band?
2 Is the singer wearing a red dress?
3 Are there two guitar players in the band?
4 Are there five trumpet players in the band?
5 Are all the band members wearing hats?

STUDENT B

UNIT 8, PAGE 79, TRAIN TO THINK

Student B

Listen to the questions your partner asks about the picture in Exercise 2. Answer with short answers. Correct the negative answers.

1 Are there eight people dancing?
2 Are the two dancing women wearing green dresses?
3 Is one dancing man wearing a blue shirt?
4 Are eight people drinking?
5 Are four people sitting down?

Acknowledgements

The authors and publishers acknowledge the following sources of copyright material and are grateful for the permissions granted. While every effort has been made, it has not always been possible to identify the sources of all the material used, or to trace all copyright holders. If any omissions are brought to our notice, we will be happy to include the appropriate acknowledgements on reprinting and in the next update to the digital edition, as applicable.

Key: U = Unit.

Photography

All the photographs are sourced from Getty Images.

U7: Erik Isakson; Matt Walford/Cultura; Alexander Spatari/Moment; bukki88/iStock/Getty Images Plus; 1001nights/E+; Ryan McVay/Allsport Concepts/Getty Images Plus; CasarsaGuru/E+; Chris Tobin/DigitalVision; miodrag ignjatovic/E+; Alistair Berg/Stone; AMR Image/iStock/Getty Images Plus; mict/E+; Michael Caulfield Archive/WireImage; monkeybusinessimages/iStock/Getty Images Plus; Adrienne Elliot/500px; Philipp Dase/EyeEm; mikroman6/Moment; Shu Xu/500px; Deborah Pendell/Moment Open; Chaay_Tee/iStock/Getty Images Plus; AntonioGuillem/iStock/Getty Images Plus; Prostock-Studio/iStock/Getty Images Plus; **U8:** RWP UK/Stone; Yuri_Arcurs/E+; Daly and Newton/The Image Bank; ginosphotos/iStock/Getty Images Plus; Maskot; Daniela Erminy/EyeEm; Xavi Torrent/Redferns; Jeremy Woodhouse/DigitalVision; Bicho_raro/iStock Editorial; guenterguni/iStock Unreleased; Gannet77/iStock Unreleased; AWL Images/Getty Images; Spanic/E+; kobbydagan/iStock Editorial; Richard Ross/The Image Bank Unreleased; Nikolay Tsuguliev/iStock/Getty Images Plus; **U9:** gilaxia/E+; Nick Bubb www.imagecaptured.co.uk/Moment; Oxana Denezhkina/Moment; milanfoto/E+; LauriPatterson/E+; Joan Ransley/Moment; kate_sept2004/E+; Hero Images/Getty Images; nitrub/iStock/Getty Images Plus; Floortje/E+; Magone/iStock/Getty Images Plus; FRANCOIS-EDMOND/iStock/Getty Images Plus; Nattawut Lakjit/EyeEm; Ikon Images/Getty Images; Lew Robertson/Stone; R.Tsubin/Moment; RedHelga/E+; Dorling Kindersley/Getty Images; p1images/iStock/Getty Images Plus; Nattaya Chanvithee/Moment; allFOOD/iStock/Getty Images Plus; subjug/iStock/Getty Images Plus; Makidotvn/iStock/Getty Images Plus; Hispanolistic/E+; Anna Bizon/EyeEm; Piotr Marcinski/EyeEm; Riccardo Botta/EyeEm; Caiaimage - Getty Images; **U10:** dzphotovideo/iStock/Getty Images Plus; Gareth; Erik Isakson; meshaphoto/E+; Rawpixel/iStock/Getty Images Plus; SCIEPRO/SCIENCE PHOTO LIBRARY/Science Photo Library; Walter Bennett/The LIFE Picture Collection; Anwar Hussein/Getty Images News; Sovfoto/Universal Images Group; Stocktrek Images; Bettmann; Ukususha/iStock/Getty Images Plus; LSOphoto/iStock/Getty Images Plus; LEON NEAL/AFP; Laurence Griffiths/Getty Images Sport; Antonio RIBEIRO/Gamma-Rapho; Tim Clayton - Corbis/Corbis Sport; Darren Gerrish/WireImage; Samir Hussein/WireImage; Steve Prezant/Image Source; SensorSpot/iStock/Getty Images Plus; **U11:** mikroman6/Moment; DrDjJanek/iStock/Getty Images Plus; Capuski/E+; Mike Wilson/500px; Jessica Lee/EyeEm; skynavin/iStock/Getty Images Plus; Samuel Moore/Moment; brackish_nz/iStock/Getty Images Plus; mark hughes/Moment; Michael Candelori/EyeEm; ddea/iStock/Getty Images Plus; Catherine Clark/www.cjdolfinphotography.co.uk/Moment; by wildestanimal/Moment; Radius Images/Getty Images; Ph. Francesco Ciccotti/Moment; Andreas Speich/EyeEm; chingting huang/iStock/Getty Images Plus; mlorenzphotography/Moment; Michael Nolan/robertharding; Sian Seabrook/500px; ©fitopardo/Moment Open; LumiNola/E+; Henn Photography/Cultura; leonid_tit/iStock/Getty Images Plus; Zinkevych/iStock/Getty Images Plus; shironosov/iStock/Getty Images Plus; monkeybusinessimages/iStock/Getty Images Plus; kristianbell/RooM; Glowimages; OJO Plus/Getty Images; CherriesJD/iStock/Getty Images Plus; Gary Chalker/Moment; **U12:** Juanpablo San Martín/Moment; Westend61; mladn61/iStock/Getty Images Plus; Pascal Forney/500px; Jungseok Park/iStock/Getty Images Plus; Michael Le/Moment; George Pachantouris/Moment; omersukrugoksu/iStock/Getty Images Plus; Ljupco/iStock/Getty Images Plus; JethuynhCan/Moment; Lisa-Blue/iStock/Getty Images Plus; CRMacedonio/Moment; Jose A. Bernat Bacete/Moment; Mark Williamson/Stockbyte; Roc Canals Photography/Moment; Tvn Phph Prung Sakdi/EyeEm; Sascha Kilmer/Moment Open; AlbertPego/iStock/Getty Images Plus; Brais Seara/Moment; Onzeg/iStock/Getty Images Plus; D.R. Hutchinson/Moment Open/Getty Images; Achim Thomae/Moment; Wildroze/E+; mantaphoto/iStock/Getty Images Plus; Shannon Miller/Moment; Melanie Hobson/EyeEm; By Eve Livesey/Moment; Gallo Images/Brand X Pictures; Tobias Schmidt/EyeEm; Paulo Amorim/Moment Open; Greg Elms/Lonely Planet Images; HAYKIRDI/iStock/Getty Images Plus; Ana Iacob/iStock Editorial/Getty Images Plus; Picture Press/Getty Images.

The following photographs are sourced from other sources/libraries.

U7: Courtesy of Maureen Beck; Copyright © Dana Mc Gregor; Mirexon/Shutterstock; Dmitry Zimin/Shutterstock; **U9**: Prarinya/Shutterstock; **U10:** Sipa/Shutterstock; Jennifer Wright/Alamy Stock Photo; Igor Stevanovic/Alamy Stock Photo.

Cover photography by Konstantin Tronin/Shutterstock; © Marco Bottigelli/Moment/Getty Images.

Illustrations

Adam Linley (Beehive Illustration) pp.82, 89, 106, 110; Mark Ruffle pp.73, 76, 94, 95, 96, 118; Martin Sanders (Beehive Illustration) pp.97; Ben Scruton (Astound US) pp.78, 79; Eszter Szepvolgyi (Beehive Illustration) pp.77.

Documentary video stills

All the video stills are sourced from Getty Images.

U7: Multi-bits/Image Bank Film; **U8:** Marco VDM/Vetta; ImagesBazaar/Photolibrary Video; **U9:** monkeybusinessimages/Creatas Video+/Getty Images Plus; **U10:** Jukin Media; BBC Universal/BBC Creative; **U11:** Ryan Gaw/Image Bank Film; **U12:** funky-data/Creatas Video; Allstar Picture Library/Photolibrary Video.

The Vlog & Grammar Rap video stills: Silversun Media Group

Audio Production: CityVox, New York

STARTER
WORKBOOK
COMBO B
with Digital Pack

CEFR
A1

AMERICAN TH!NK

SECOND EDITION

Herbert Puchta,
Jeff Stranks &
Peter Lewis-Jones
with Vicki Anderson

CAMBRIDGE
UNIVERSITY PRESS

This page is intentionally left blank.

CONTENTS

7 LIVING FOR SPORTS

GRAMMAR
can (ability)

→ SB p.68

1 ★☆☆ Match the sentences with the pictures. Write 1–8 in the boxes.

1 He can ride a bike.
2 They can sing.
3 They can swim.
4 We can dance.
5 We can't dance.
6 He can't swim.
7 They can't sing.
8 He can't ride a bike.

A

E

B

F

C

G

D

H

2 ★★☆ Match the questions and answers.

0 Can you and Jayden sing? *e*
1 Can you speak Italian? ☐
2 Can David play the violin? ☐
3 Can Helen cook? ☐
4 Can a Ferrari go fast? ☐
5 Can Karim and Jake ride a bike? ☐

a No, he can't.
b Yes, they can.
c Yes, I can.
d Yes, it can.
e No, we can't.
f Yes, she can.

3 ★★★ Write sentences with *can* and *can't*.

0 I / ride a bike (✓) / roller-skate (✗)
I can ride a bike, but I can't roller-skate.

1 I / sing (✓) / dance (✗)
______

2 my little sister / talk (✗) / walk (✓)
______

3 they / speak Spanish (✓) / speak Turkish (✗)
______

4 my brother / drive (✗) / cook (✓)
______

5 we / jump high (✗) / run fast (✓)
______

6 my grandmother / play the piano (✗) / play the guitar (✓)
______

7 birds / sing (✓) / talk (✗)
______

PRONUNCIATION
Vowel sound /ɔː/ Go to page 120.

4 ★★★ **Look at the pictures and write questions with *can*. Then answer them so they are true for you.**

0 
Can you drive?
No, I can't.

1 
____
____

2 
____
____

3 
____
____

4 
____
____

5 ★★★ **Complete the sentences with your own ideas.**

1 I can't ________________,
but I can ________________.
2 My best friend can ________________,
but he/she can't ________________.
3 My teacher can't ________________,
but he/she can ________________.
4 Babies can ________________,
but they can't ________________.
5 My mom can ________________,
but she can't ________________.
6 My dad can't ________________,
but he can ________________.
7 The cat can ________________,
but it can't ________________.

Prepositions of time

→ SB p.71

6 ★☆☆ **Circle the correct options.**

0 I leave home (*at*) / *in* / *on* 7 a.m. to go to school.
1 Julieta's birthday is *at* / *in* / *on* May.
2 The game starts *at* / *in* / *on* 8 p.m.
3 It's very hot *at* / *in* / *on* the summer.
4 I don't go to school *at* / *in* / *on* Sundays.
5 There's a holiday *at* / *in* / *on* April 7th this year.
6 We play volleyball *at* / *in* / *on* Friday afternoons.
7 The first day of school is *at* / *in* / *on* the fall.

7 ★★☆ **Complete the sentences with *at*, *in*, or *on*.**

0 The party is on Saturday ___*at*___ 7 p.m.
1 School starts ________ 8 a.m., and it finishes ________ 3 p.m.
2 It's not very cold ________ the spring.
3 My school break starts ________ June and finishes ________ September.
4 My birthday is ________ April 1st. It's ________ the spring. This year it's ________ a Monday.

8 ★★☆ **Write the words in the correct columns.**

Friday | ~~May~~ | May 22nd | midnight | night | noon | September | seven o'clock | the evening | the morning | Tuesday | 3:30 p.m. | July 7th

in	on	at
May		

GET IT RIGHT!

Prepositions of time

We use *on* for days of the week and dates.
✓ *I go swimming on Saturday.*
✗ *I go swimming ~~in~~ Saturday.*
✓ *Her birthday is on May 1st.*
✗ *Her birthday is ~~in~~ May 1st.*
We use *at* for clock times.
✓ *My dance lesson is at five o'clock.*
✗ *My dance lesson is ~~on~~ five o'clock.*
We use *in* for months and seasons.
✓ *Is your birthday in November?*
✗ *Is your birthday ~~at~~ November?*
✓ *We often go to the beach in the summer.*
✗ *We often go to the beach ~~at~~ the summer.*

Complete the sentences with *at*, *in*, or *on*.

0 I will be there ___*on*___ Sunday evening.
1 He wants to have a party ________ July 7th.
2 I can come ________ Monday or Friday.
3 My school exams are ________ June.
4 Can you meet me ________ ten thirty?
5 The trees are pretty ________ the fall.
6 It starts ________ a quarter to eight.

VOCABULARY

Sports

→ SB p.68

1 ★★★ **Look at the pictures and write sentences.**

Carlo

Lewis

Megan

Adam

Liz

Ethan

Amelia

Marta

0 *Carlo skis.*
1 ______
2 ______
3 ______
4 ______
5 ______
6 ______
7 ______

Telling the time

→ SB p.69

2 ★★☆ **Write the times under the clocks.**

0 *It's seven o'clock.*

3 ______

1 ______

4 ______

2 ______

5 ______

Months and seasons

→ SB p.71

3 ★★☆ **Complete the months and seasons with the missing consonants.**

Months

1 O _ _ o _ e _
2 _ u _ e
3 A _ _ i _
4 _ e _ e _ _ e _
5 _ a _
6 _ u _ _
7 _ a _ u a _ _
8 A u _ u _ _
9 _ e _ _ e _ _ e _
10 _ o _ e _ _ e _
11 _ e _ _ u a _ _
12 _ a _ _ _

Seasons

13 _ u _ _ e _
14 f _ l _
15 _ _ _ i _ _
16 _ i _ _ e _

4 ★★★ **Choose four months. Say what season they are in and what you do in each month.**

0 *August is in the summer. I go on vacation with my family in August.*
1 ______
2 ______
3 ______
4 ______

Ordinal numbers

→ SB p.71

5 ★☆☆ **Complete the table.**

1st	*first*	9th	
	second	10th	
3rd			eleventh
4th		12th	
	fifth		thirteenth
6th		20th	
7th		30th	
8th			thirty-first

6 ★★☆ **Write the ordinal numbers.**

0 14th *fourteenth*
1 21st ______
2 27th ______
3 22nd ______
4 28th ______
5 15th ______
6 16th ______
7 23rd ______
8 29th ______
9 24th ______
10 17th ______
11 18th ______
12 19th ______
13 26th ______
14 25th ______

REFERENCE

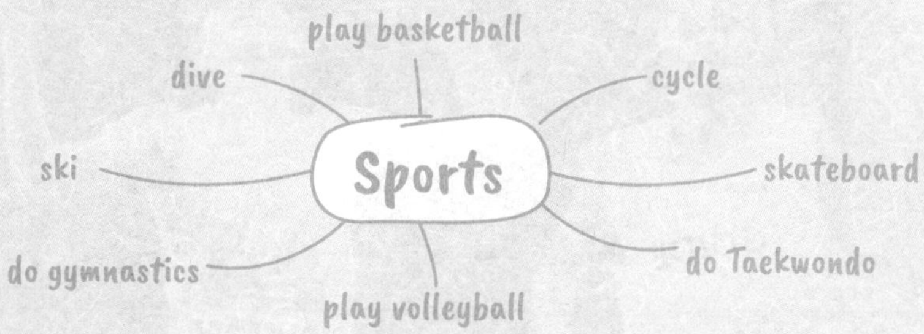

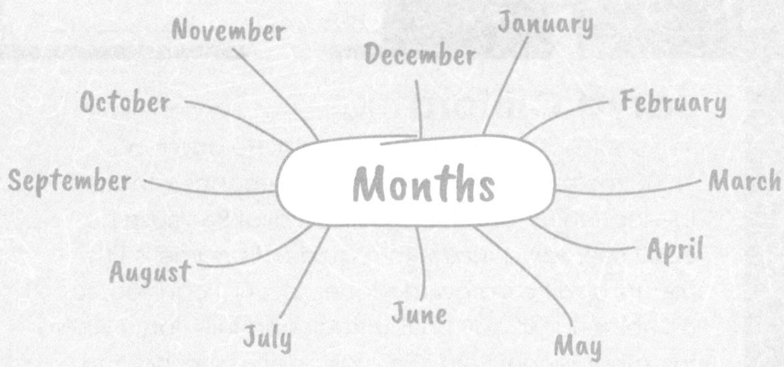

Telling the time

1 It's three o'clock.

2 It's eight thirty.

3 It's a quarter after ten.

4 It's a quarter to one.

Ordinal numbers

1st – first	5th – fifth	9th – ninth	13th – thirteenth
2nd – second	6th – sixth	10th – tenth	20th – twentieth
3rd – third	7th – seventh	11th – eleventh	30th – thirtieth
4th – fourth	8th – eighth	12th – twelfth	31st – thirty-first

VOCABULARY *EXTRA*

1 **Match the objects in the pictures with the sports from the list.**

badminton | foosball | frisbee | karate | netball | running

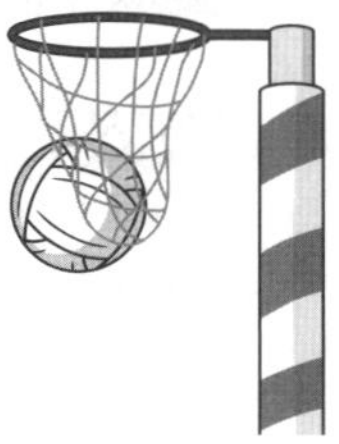
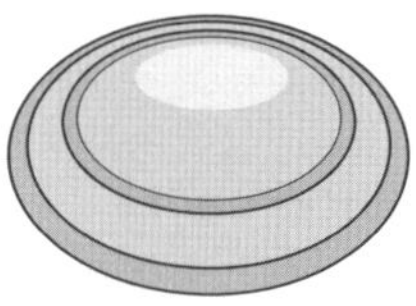

1 ____________ 2 ____________ 3 ____________ 4 ____________ 5 ____________ 6 ____________

2 **Complete the sentences with the correct sport from Exercise 1.**

1 We often play ________________ at the café near my house.
2 Girls at my school play ________________ . It's a little like basketball.
3 To go ________________ , all you need is a pair of sneakers.
4 When you play ________________ , you use a racket, but not a ball.
5 I do ________________ , a Japanese martial art.
6 A lot of people play ________________ in the park.

SPORTS FOR ALL

The Paralympic Games are a big sporting event for athletes with disabilities. The Games show the world all the amazing things that these athletes can do. They take place every two years: after the Summer Olympics and after the Winter Olympics. Here are two incredible Paralympians.

This is [3]______________ .
He's from [4]______________ .

Jessica Long is American. Jessica has no legs below the knee, but she's a fantastic swimmer. She can swim really fast using only her arms and body. She's a very successful Paralympian. She has a lot of gold medals from several different Paralympic Games! Jessica loves sports and also plays basketball and goes ice-skating, cycling, and rock-climbing. Another interesting fact about Jessica is her birthday. It's February 29th – this happens only every four years!

Jaryd Clifford is Australian. He can't see very well, but he can run really fast. He can run 1,500 meters in 3 minutes and 47 seconds – that's in the top ten for *all* athletes in Australia! Because he can't see, Jaryd runs with a guide. His name is Tim Logan, and he's a good runner, too. Tim can see, so he helps Jaryd stay on the track and tells Jaryd where the other runners are. Tim is also Jaryd's friend and knows him well, so they are a good team. Jaryd is young, but he's already very successful. He has a lot of medals, including a gold one and a world record. He wants to get even better in the future!

This is [1]______________ .
She's from [2]______________ .

READING

1 **Read the text and complete the sentences under the pictures.**

2 **Read the text again and answer the questions.**

1 When do the Paralympics happen? ______________
2 How does Jessica swim? ______________
3 Does Jessica have medals from more than one Paralympics? ______________
4 What is different about Jessica's birthday? ______________
____
5 What can't Jaryd Clifford do? ______________
6 How does he stay on the track? ______________
7 Why are Jaryd and Tim a good team? ______________
____

3 CRITICAL THINKING **Read the information about the athletes. Is each sentence about Jessica (JL) or Jaryd (JC) ?**

1 __________ can win races with athletes who don't have disabilities.
2 __________ spends a lot of time doing different sports.
3 __________ has a lot of gold medals from many different Paralympic Games.
4 A good friend helps __________ to be an amazing athlete.
5 __________ doesn't have a birthday every year.
6 __________ has a world record.

DEVELOPING Writing

An amazing person

1 INPUT **Read the text. What sport is mentioned?**

MY AMAZING GRANDMA

My grandma Ana is an amazing person. We live in the same city, San Diego, so I see her a lot. She's 72 years old, and she still swims every day. She's on a team at a swimming club and does races most weekends. She swims in special races for people over 65. She always wins. She's really fast. She can swim 400 meters in five minutes. She loves swimming. It makes her feel young. I like her because she's a great swimmer, she's fun, and she makes really good cookies!

2 ANALYZE **Imagine you're the writer of the text and answer the questions.**

0 Who is she?
My grandma Ana.

1 Where does she live?
____

2 What does she do?
____

3 What amazing things can she do?
____

4 Why do you like her?
____

3 PLAN **Make notes about an amazing person you know.**

1 Who is he/she?
____

2 Where does he/she live?
____

3 How old is he/she?
____

4 What amazing things can he/she do?
____

5 Why do you like him/her?
____

WRITING TIP: Third person "s" for *he, she,* and *it*

In English it's easy to forget the "s" at the end of verbs in the third person singular!

She swims every day.
She does races.
It makes her feel young.

4 PRODUCE **Use your answers to the questions in Exercise 3 to write a short text about your person. Write about 60 words.**

____

LISTENING

1 7.03 **Listen and match the conversations with the pictures. Write 1–3 in the boxes.**

A ☐

B ☐

C ☐

2 7.03 **Listen again and draw the times on the clocks.**

Conversation 1:
What time do they play tennis?

Conversation 2:
What time is the movie they choose?

Conversation 3:
What time do they meet?

3 7.03 **Listen again and complete each sentence with one word.**

0 Louise feels a little *bored*.
1 Louise is __________ until 1 p.m.
2 Rosie wants to go to the movies in the __________.
3 The first movie is at __________ thirty.
4 Lucy wants to go __________ with Dan.
5 Lucy finishes __________ at five.

DIALOGUE

4 **Put the conversation in order.**

☐	**Ben**	We can't. We don't have a frisbee.
☐	**Ben**	Videos! That's why I'm bored. I'm tired of watching videos.
☐	**Ben**	We can't. She's on vacation.
1	**Ben**	I'm bored. What can we do?
☐	**Selma**	Is she? So how about some more videos?
☐	**Selma**	Why don't we play frisbee?
☐	**Selma**	No frisbee? OK, let's go to Eva's house.

PHRASES FOR FLUENCY → SB p.72

5 **Match the questions with the answers.**

0 Are these your things? *c*
1 Oh, no, look at the rain. ☐
2 Where's Cape Town? ☐
3 Look, there goes the bus. Now what? ☐

a It's no big deal. I have an umbrella.
b I'm sure it's in South Africa.
c No, I think that's Dean's stuff.
d Don't worry. There's another one in 15 minutes.

6 **Complete the dialogue with the words and phrases that are underlined in Exercise 5.**

Mom Come on, Owen. It's time for school.
Owen I'm ready, Mom.
Mom Do you have your swimming [0] *stuff*?
Owen I don't have a swimming lesson today.
Mom [1] __________ you do, Owen. It's Thursday.
Owen Thursday! Oh, no. I have a swimming lesson! But my towel's wet. [2] __________?
Mom [3] __________. You can take another towel.
Owen Thanks, Mom. You're the best!

SUM IT UP

1 **Read and write the names of the sports.**

Welcome to a day of **sports** on BCB TV.

We've got a great show of sports action for you this Saturday.

We have live  [0] *soccer* from Anfield, where Liverpool plays Manchester City in the big game.

We have  [1] ________________ with ALL the action from the NBA.

There's  [2] ________________ from last night's game between Brazil and China.

There's live  [3] ________________ from the World Championships in Copenhagen.

And we have  [4] ________________ from the Alpine World Cup, this weekend in Croatia.

There's something for everyone!

2 **Read the clues and complete the TV sports programs.**

Start time	Finish time	Sports program
1 p.m.	*1:30 p.m.*	
p.m.	p.m.	
p.m.	p.m.	
p.m.	p.m.	
p.m.	p.m.	

1 The afternoon of sports starts at 1 p.m.
2 Gymnastics is the fourth program.
3 The skiing is on for half an hour.
4 Soccer is after volleyball.
5 Basketball starts six hours after skiing finishes.
6 The soccer starts at 3 p.m.
7 Gymnastics is on for two and a half hours.
8 Volleyball is on for an hour and a half.
9 There are eight hours of sports.
10 Skiing is the first sport.
11 The last show is 90 minutes long.

3 **Put the words in the list into four categories. There are three words in each category. Name the categories.**

~~August~~ | cycling | fifth | first | June | May | snowboarding | spring | summer | Taekwondo | third | winter

1 *MONTHS*	2	3	4
August			

8 FEEL THE RHYTHM

Grammar rap!

GRAMMAR
Present continuous

→ SB p.76

1 ★☆☆ Circle the correct options.

0 She isn't here. She ('s) / 're skateboarding in the park.
1 What *is* / *are* you doing?
2 Sorry, I can't talk now. I *'m* / *is* watching a movie.
3 All my friends are here. We *'s* / *'re* having a great time!
4 My brother's in his room. He *'s* / *'re* playing computer games.
5 My mom and dad *is* / *are* shopping at the supermarket.
6 I think they're happy. They *'s* / *'re* smiling a lot!
7 Look! There's Zack. Where *'s* / *'re* he going?

2 ★☆☆ Write the *-ing* form of these verbs.

0 shop ___*shopping*___
1 play ______
2 give ______
3 sit ______
4 dance ______
5 smile ______
6 run ______
7 walk ______
8 read ______
9 take ______
10 try ______
11 stop ______
12 write ______
13 draw ______

3 ★★☆ Complete the sentences with the present continuous form of the verbs in parentheses.

0 Go away, Li. I ___*'m not talking*___ to you! (not talk)
1 Let's go for a walk. It ______ . (not rain)
2 ______ you ______ the party? (enjoy)
3 ______ your brother ______ a good time in college? (have)
4 What ______ you ______ , Joaquim? (do)
5 The TV is on, but they ______ it. (not watch)
6 Ivy! You ______ to me! (not listen)
7 What ______ the cat ______ ? (eat)
8 They ______ well today. (not play)

4 ★★☆ Lily is telling Juan about a new game show on TV. Complete the conversation with the present continuous form of the verbs in parentheses.

Lily Hey, Juan, how are you? Are you free this evening?
Juan Hmm, I'm not sure. Why?
Lily Well, there's a great new game show on TV. There are two teams. When it starts, a player on one team [0] ___*is watching*___ (watch) a video on a tablet. Of course, the other players can't see what [1] ______ (happen) on the screen.
Juan So?
Lily Well, the player with the tablet says things like, "A boy [2] ______ (run). He [3] ______ (wear) shorts. He [4] ______ (hold) a ball." After each sentence, the other players guess what [5] ______ (happen) in the video.
Juan And then what?
Lily The players can ask ten questions.
Juan Like, "What [6] ______ they ______ (do) in the video?"
Lily No, of course not. They can only ask questions like, "[7] ______ the boy ______ (play) with friends?" or "[8] ______ they ______ (go) to school?" or "[9] ______ they ______ (watch) a game of soccer?"
Juan And then?
Lily Sometimes the player watching the video says what [10] ______ (not happen) in the video. Things like, "The boy [11] ______ (not sitting) on the floor," or "The people [12] ______ (not play) music." And the other player gets a point if they can say what's happening in the video.
Juan Hmm. I don't like watching game shows. I like watching movies.
Lily Oh. Well, please watch tonight. There's a surprise for you!
Juan A surprise? For me? Now I want to watch it!

5 ★★★ **Complete this extract from the game show with the correct form of the verbs in the list.**

hit | hold | kick | not go | not smile
not throw | play (x3) | stand | ~~wear~~

Host Let's play! Lily, you have the tablet, so your team starts.

Lily Well, I can see 12 girls here. They [0] *'re wearing* shorts and T-shirts.

Simon [1] ________ they ________ a game?

Lily Yes, they are. They [2] ________ with a ball.

Keiko [3] ________ they ________ the ball with their feet?

Lily No, they aren't. And they [4] ________ the ball. One girl [5] ________ the ball in her hand. She [6] ________ behind a line on the floor.

Paulo [7] ________ she ________ the ball with her hand?

Lily Yes, she is. But the ball [8] ________ into the net. That's not good. She isn't happy. She [9] ________ .

Keiko I know! [10] ________ they ________ volleyball?

Lily Yes, they are!

Host Great job! That's one point to you.

6 ★★★ **What do you think your family and friends are doing now? Look at the example and write similar sentences about them.**

0 *I think my sister is reading a magazine now.*
1 ________
2 ________
3 ________
4 ________
5 ________

like / don't like + -ing

→ SB p.78

7 ★★☆ **Write sentences with the correct form of the verbs.**

0 I / like / read / long books
I like reading long books.
1 my sister / not like / do / gymnastics
____
2 my parents / hate / watch / scary movies
____
3 my best friend / like / listen to / classical music
____
4 I / not like / go to / buy clothes
____
5 I / love / read / in bed
____

8 ★★☆ **Complete the text. Use *love* (☺☺), *like* (☺), *don't/doesn't like* (☹), *hate* (☹☹), and the correct form of the verbs.**

My family is a little strange – they like or don't like all kinds of different things. My sister [0] *doesn't like cooking* (☹ cook), but she [1] ________ (☺☺ clean) her room. My father [2] ________ (☹☹ go) for walks, but he [3] ________ (☺ take) exercise classes at the gym. My mother [4] ________ (☺ read) books, but she [5] ________ (☹☹ look) at magazines. My parents [6] ________ (☺☺ travel) to other countries, but they [7] ________ (☹ speak) other languages. And me? Well, I just [8] ________ (☺☺ be) with my strange family!

9 ★★☆ **Complete the sentences so they are true for you.**

0 I love *singing in the shower* and *dancing in my bedroom* .
1 I love ________ and ________ .
2 I like ________ and ________ .
3 I don't like ________ and ________ .
4 I hate ________ and ________ .

GET IT RIGHT!

Present continuous

We use subject + *am/is/are* + *-ing* form of the main verb.

✓ *We are watching a video.*
✗ *~~We watching~~ a video.*
✓ *I am eating a sandwich.*
✗ *~~I am eat~~ a sandwich.*

Complete the sentences with the correct present continuous form of the verbs in parentheses.

0 She *is taking* (take) some photos of her food.
1 We ________ (do) the shopping at the moment.
2 ________ (you / listen) to rap music?
3 He ________ (wear) a red shirt and black pants.
4 They ________ (walk) to the sports center.
5 Who ________ (play) computer games?
6 He ________ (not eat) a sandwich; he's eating cake!

VOCABULARY

Present continuous verbs

→ SB p.76

1 ★☆☆ **Look at the picture above and complete the sentences with the correct form of the verbs from the list.**

cheer | dance | leave | read | ~~run~~ | sing
sit | smile | stand | take | talk | wear

0 Pierre is *running* .
1 Elena is ________ .
2 Charlie is ________ .
3 Lucy is ________ on a bench.
4 Lucas and Kerry are ________ .
5 Callum is ________ a hat.
6 Helena is ________ .
7 Rob is ________ .
8 Claire is ________ on her phone.
9 Matt is ________ a photo.
10 Fiona is ________ .
11 Jen and Pablo are ________ the park.

2 ★★☆ **Complete each sentence with a verb from Exercise 1. Use the correct form of the verbs.**

0 I'm *reading* a really good book. It's very interesting!
1 My dad's crazy. He wants to ________ a marathon.
2 Let's ________ a song.
3 This train ________ at 10:45 and arrives in Atlanta at 12:40.
4 Look at Mike! He's ________ green pants and a purple sweater!
5 Can you ________ a photo of us, please?
6 I love ________ on the phone with my friends.
7 This is my favorite chair. I love ________ here.

Clothes

→ SB p.79

3 ★★☆ **Find 11 more clothes items in the word search.**

P	R	O	U	D	E	D	J	A	N	S	T
A	(S	H	I	R	T)	R	A	S	E	H	P
N	A	T	H	L	O	E	W	K	S	I	O
T	R	E	A	I	N	S	X	C	R	R	R
S	N	A	E	J	O	S	H	O	E	S	E
H	T	L	O	T	S	A	U	S	S	W	T
E	R	B	K	R	H	B	N	Y	B	E	A
R	I	R	W	E	O	U	K	J	P	A	E
L	H	A	D	I	R	Y	L	U	R	F	W
P	S	C	O	A	T	T	R	N	Z	E	S
J	T	R	I	K	S	G	E	S	A	R	M
U	M	B	E	S	R	E	K	A	E	N	S

4 ★★☆ **(Circle) the odd one out in each list.**

0 (jeans) sweater shirt
1 socks sneakers coat
2 shorts T-shirt pants
3 dress skirt shoes
4 sweater T-shirt coat

5 ★★★ **Write answers to the questions so they are true for you.**

1 What clothes do you love wearing on the weekend?
____

2 What clothes do you never buy?
____

3 Of all the people you know, who wears really nice clothes? What do they wear?
____

PRONUNCIATION
Intonation – listing items Go to page 120.

REFERENCE

Verbs

base form	*-ing* form
cheer	cheering
dance	dancing
leave	leaving
read	reading
run	running
sing	singing
sit	sitting
smile	smiling
stand	standing
take	taking
talk	talking
wear	wearing

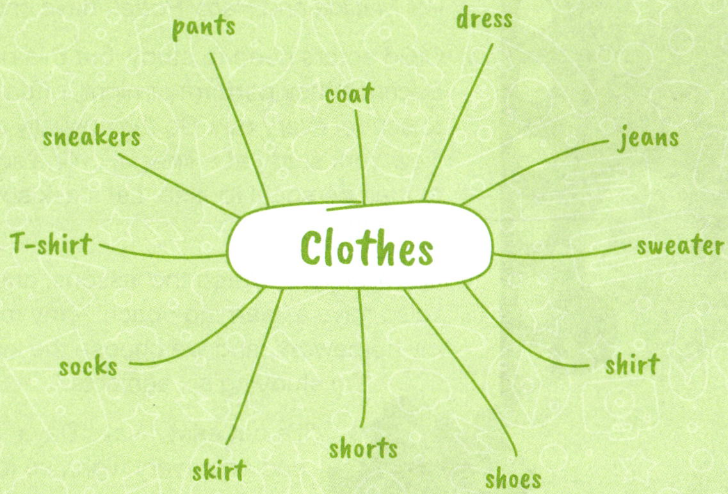

VOCABULARY *EXTRA*

1 Label the picture with the words from the list of clothes.

handbag | necklace | raincoat | suit | tie | umbrella

2 Complete the sentences with words from the list in Exercise 1.

1 Our school uniform has black pants, a white shirt, and a red ___________ .

2 It's raining! You need to wear your ___________ and take an ___________ .

3 Gio's dad doesn't want to wear a ___________ every day to work. He likes jeans and T-shirts!

4 "That's a beautiful ___________ ."
"It's a birthday present for my sister. It's gold."

5 "Oh, no! I can't find my ___________ . My new phone's in it."
"Don't worry, Mom. It's on the sofa."

In theaters around the world, musicals are very popular. And some shows, like *Matilda* and *Harry Potter*, have child actors. So what are their lives like?

Child actors need to study, but this doesn't mean they go to school. Because they perform at night, often until late, it's difficult for them to go to school every day. So they usually study at home. Many child actors in New York study at a special online school. They can add virtual lessons to their personal routine. Let's ask some child actors in a New York show about it!

Gabbi says, "I watch the lessons, and I can talk to the teachers online. I also have a 'learning coach' – my mom! She helps me study and do my homework, and we choose the lessons together. At the moment, I'm studying six subjects."

"It's not easy," says Daya. "There is a show most afternoons and one every night, so it's difficult to do all the work the teachers give us and get good grades. I am not in every show, though (two other girls play the same part as me), and that way we all have time for schoolwork and other things – I'm also taking dancing and singing lessons. The other girls aren't doing that, but they love playing video games and reading."

Online learning is also good because child actors sometimes move around. Daya explains, "My play isn't showing in New York at the moment. We're touring the US and Canada with the show, and we're studying for school exams. We stay in each town for a week, in a hotel. It's a great life! We love it!"

READING

1 **Read the article about child actors. Do they work all the time? What else do they do?**

2 **Read the article again and mark the sentences T (true) or F (false). Correct the false statements.**

0 Musicals aren't popular around the world. [F]
They are very popular.

1 Child actors all have to continue their education. [ ]
______

2 Theater shows never finish late. [ ]
______

3 All New York child actors study online. [ ]
______

4 They talk to the teachers by phone. [ ]
______

5 When you're in a play, there are often two shows a day. [ ]
______

6 Three different children sometimes play the same part. [ ]
______

7 Daya is performing in New York now. [ ]
______

3 CRITICAL THINKING **Imagine you are a child actor in the theater. What do you like about it? What don't you like about it? Why? Use ideas from this list or your own ideas. Write sentences.**

- getting up early / going to bed late
- organizing your day
- schoolwork and homework
- having fun with friends

______
______
______
______
______
______
______
______
______
______
______

Describing a scene

1 INPUT **Read Dalia's email. Why is everyone busy?**

Elias
Dalia@thinkmail.com

Hi Elias,

It's Sunday morning. The sun is shining. I'm sitting in my room. I love sitting here. It's usually quiet, and I like watching the birds in my backyard. But the yard is busy today. My parents are having a big party to celebrate being married for 25 years!!

There's a big tent in the yard. We're having lunch in the tent. My parents are moving tables and chairs. They're laughing and making a lot of noise. There are some people walking into the kitchen. They are carrying big boxes of food and drinks for the party. Uh oh! Now my dad's calling me. He's choosing the party music. His favorite songs are really old, so he wants me to help him!

What are you doing today?

Dalia

2 ANALYZE **Match the parts of the phrases. Then read the email again and check your answers.**

0 watching — b
1 choosing
2 having
3 moving
4 carrying

a big boxes
b the birds
c party music
d tables and chairs
e a party

3 PLAN **Imagine it's Sunday morning. Use the ideas below and make notes.**

a Choose a place:
- the shopping center
- your house
- the beach
- another place

b What are you doing? What's happening near you? Who can you see and what are they doing? Use these verbs to help you.

buy | have | listen | play | read | sit | watch

____
____
____
____
____
____

c Something happens – it changes things. What happens?

____
____
____
____
____
____

4 PRODUCE **Use your notes to write an email to a friend about your Sunday morning. Use the email in Exercise 1 to help you. Write about 60 words.**

____
____
____
____
____
____
____
____
____
____
____
____
____
____

WRITING TIP: Starting an email

Start with *Hi* + your friend's name and a comma (,). Then start the email on the next line.

LISTENING

1 8.02 **Listen to a boy calling his sister and choose the correct answer.**

1 Right now, he is in the hotel *bedroom / lobby.*

2 After the call, he is going to *Buckingham Palace / the theater.*

2 8.02 **Listen again and complete the sentences with one word.**

0 Ricky's sister's name is *Petra* .

1 Ricky is on a class trip to ________ .

2 From his hotel room, he can see some girls riding ________ .

3 He can see a couple wearing formal ________ .

4 His sister thinks the couple is going to the ________ .

5 She forgets that Ricky is going see *The Lion King* ________ .

6 Ricky is wearing nice ________ and his best blue ________ .

7 Petra wants Ricky to call her again ________ .

DIALOGUE

3 8.03 **Listen to Stefan interviewing Alicia for a school project. How many questions does he ask her?**

____

4 8.03 **Listen again and complete the conversation.**

Stefan Hi, Alicia! I'd like to ask you some questions. Is that OK?

Alicia Yeah, sure. What about?

Stefan What do you like doing in the evenings?

Alicia You mean, after school? Well, I like [0] *chatting with friends online* , and I love [1] ________ .

Stefan And what about the weekends?

Alicia On Saturdays, I help clean the house. I like [2] ________ , but I hate [3] ________ the dishes. And on Sundays, I like [4] ________ with my friends at the park or [5] ________ to the movies.

Stefan Thanks, Alicia. Now I can finish my school project.

Alicia Good thing! It's only ten minutes until class!

5 **Now Stefan is interviewing his grandpa. Put Grandpa's answers in the correct order.**

Stefan Grandpa, can I ask you some questions, please?

Grandpa Yes, of course. What do you want to know?

Stefan Well, what do you like doing in the evenings?

Grandpa [0] movies / I / watching / love / .
I love watching movies.

Stefan And what about the weekends?

Grandpa [1] On / I / at / the / soccer club / Saturdays, / like / friends / meeting / my / .
____

[2] I / On / visit / usually / house / Sundays, / your / .
____

[3] family / seeing / I / my / love / .
____

[4] I / don't / your music / listening / like / to / But / always / .
____

Stefan Thanks a lot, Grandpa.

6 **Imagine that Stefan is interviewing you. Complete the answers to his questions so they are true for you.**

Stefan What do you like doing in the evenings?

You I like ________ , and I love ________ .

Stefan What about the weekend?

You On Saturdays, I like ________ , and on Sundays, I like ________ .

Stefan What do you hate doing?

You I hate ________ .

Stefan And what are you doing now?

You I'm ________ .

Train to THINK

Memorizing

7 8.02 **Listen to Ricky and Petra again. Read the questions (1–5) that Petra asks Ricky. Can you remember Ricky's answers to the questions? Write them down.**

1 How's your class trip going?
________ !

2 What's your room like?
________ !

3 What are you doing now?
________ .

4 What are you doing tonight?
Petra, ________ , remember?

5 Are you wearing a suit, ha ha?
What ________ ?
________ !

8 8.02 **Listen one more time and check your answers.**

TOWARDS A2 Key for Schools

EXAM SKILLS: READING

Answering multiple-choice questions

1 Read Monika's email to her friend Paulo and answer the questions.

1 Where is Monika? ________________

2 What does she want to see there? ________________

Paulo
Monika@thinkmail.com

Hi Paulo,

How are you? I'm on holiday – well, you know that, right? – and I'm having a great time here in Granada. We're staying in a nice hotel near the city centre. It's small, but it's cheap and very comfortable, and we like it. The people who work here speak good English. That's great, because my family doesn't speak Spanish! Well, I know a few words now – *gracias* and *por favor*, that kind of thing! I can say *Tengo hambre*, too. That means 'I'm hungry', and you know me, I'm always hungry!

Granada is a cool place. The famous Alhambra palace is here. It's very beautiful. And it's a great place for Flamenco, too. I love Flamenco dancing and I want to see some here. Oh, just a minute – my mum says that Dad is on his tablet and he's getting tickets for a Flamenco show tonight here in the city! Great!

Hope you're well. Please write soon, OK?

Monika

2 Read the email again. Choose the correct answers (A, B or C).

0 Monika's family are staying in a __________ hotel.
A big (B) comfortable C expensive

1 The people at the hotel __________ English.
A like B don't understand C understand

2 Monika knows __________ words in Spanish.
A some B a lot of C no

3 In Granada there is a famous __________ .
A palace B dance clubs C cool place

4 Monika's __________ has a tablet.
A father B mother C Flamenco

5 Monika's father __________ a Flamenco show.
A isn't getting tickets for B is buying tickets for C is reading a book about

READING TIP

When the questions about a text are multiple choice, it means you have to choose the one correct answer from three or four possibilities.

- Look for items that are grammatically wrong. For example, in the following question, A is wrong because we can't have 'a' before a vowel, and C is wrong because we can't use 'some' before a singular noun.

  He's eating __________ apple.

  A a B an C some
- Look for words that have similar meanings. For example, in Question 5 of Exercise 2, 'buying' and 'getting' have the same meaning.
- You must check all three (or four) options before you decide which one is correct.

CONSOLIDATION

LISTENING

1 8.04 **Listen to Daniela and circle the correct answers (A, B, or C).**

1 Daniela's birthday is …
A October 20th.
B October 21st.
C October 1st.

2 Daniela's camera is a present from …
A her grandparents.
B her brother.
C her mother and father.

3 Daniela's favorite season is …
A winter.
B fall.
C summer.

2 8.04 **Listen again and complete the words.**

1 Daniela is f__________ .
2 She thinks Ipswich isn't e__________ .
3 Daniela is taking d__________ lessons.
4 Daniela has special s__________ for dancing.
5 Daniela's friends like s__________ .
6 Daniela likes w__________ on cold days.

GRAMMAR

3 Circle the correct options.

Bella Hi, Kurt. What [1]*are / is* you doing?

Kurt Oh, hi, Bella. [2]*I wait / I'm waiting* for my dad. And you?

Bella I'm doing some shopping. I'm not [3]*buying / buy* much – just some stuff for school. Hey, you have new headphones. They look great!

Kurt Yeah, thanks! [4]*I'm listening / I listen* to a lot of music. Waiting is boring! I [5]*can't / don't can* wait without music!

Bella What [6]*do you listen / are you listening* to right now?

Kurt It's some violin music. I really like [7]*listen / listening* to violin music.

Bella [8]*Can you / Do you can* play the violin, Kurt?

Kurt No, I [9]*can't / can*. But I often [10]*listen / am listening* to it!

4 Charlie is showing Eva a video on his phone. Put the words in order to make sentences.

0 is / Liam / brother / This / my / .
This is my brother Liam.
1 an old people's home / He's / arriving at / .
____
2 meeting / He / his friends / is / .
____
3 Liam's / today / the guitar / his friends / playing /with / .
____
4 are / at the old people's home / They / giving / a concert / .
____
5 a chair / is / on / Liam / sitting / .
____
6 next to / is / him / My friend Amanda / standing / .
____
7 Beatles / singing / songs / They're / old / .
____
8 are / The / with / them / old people / singing / .
____

VOCABULARY

5 Put the words from the list into three groups. Give each group a title. Then write one more word in each group.

August | dress | February | golf | gymnastics | jeans
sweater | June | May | sneakers | surfing | tennis

1 *months*	2	3

6 Complete the sentences with the words from the list. There are two extra words.

cheer | dance | dancing | second
summer | talk | two | watching

1 My birthday is the __________ of March.
2 I have a problem with my foot, so I can't __________ tonight.
3 Every week, I __________ to my grandparents in Mexico on the phone.
4 I like listening to music, but I don't like __________ to it!
5 We always __________ when our team wins.
6 It's great here in the __________ when the weather is hot.

DIALOGUE

7 8.05 **Put the conversations in order. Then listen and check.**

Conversation 1

☐ **Erin** Great idea! I love baking. Let's check that we have everything we need.
☐ **Erin** No, it's five o'clock. The stores close at five thirty.
☐ **Erin** I'm really bored.
☐ **Dana** Me, too. Why don't we go into town? We can go shopping.
☐ **Dana** Oh yes! OK, how about making a cake?

Conversation 2

☐ **Rico** OK, it's no big deal. We can stay here in my house. I have a good book to read.
☐ **Rico** Hey, how about going for a walk?
☐ **Rico** Yes, I'm sure I can find one for you.
☐ **Sara** Great idea! I love reading. Do you have a book for me, too?
☐ **Sara** No thanks! It's cold outside. And I don't like walking very much.

READING

8 **Read the phone conversation. Then complete the sentences with the correct information.**

Noah Hey, Ella, what are you doing?
Ella I'm talking to you on the phone, ha ha!
Noah Yes, very funny. But seriously – what are you doing?
Ella Nothing really. I'm just sitting in my room. Why?
Noah How about coming to the park? That's where I am now!
Ella The park? Why? What's happening in the park?
Noah There's a race today. It's a ten-kilometer run. My parents are running in it.
Ella Are they crazy? It's winter! It's cold, and it's raining.
Noah It isn't raining very much. And I'm wearing a warm coat and shoes. So, I'm OK.
Ella Well, no thanks. I like being warm, not cold.
Noah OK, it's no big deal. Oh, and Mark Watson's running in the race. I can see him, too.
Ella Really? Mark Watson from our school?
Noah Yes, him. And at the moment, he's first – he's winning!
Ella Right, I'm putting my coat on, and I'm leaving the house now.
Noah Really?
Ella Yes – Mark Watson's there, so I want to be there, too!
Noah Oh, OK. See you soon then!

1 Ella is in ________________ .
2 Noah is in ________________ .
3 There's a ________________-kilometer race today.
4 Noah's ________________ and ________________ are running in the race.
5 Noah ________________ cold because he's ________________ a warm coat.
6 Ella doesn't like ________________ .
7 Mark Watson is a boy from their ________________ .
8 Mark is ________________ the race.
9 Ella is ________________ the house because she wants to ________________ .

WRITING

9 **Write a short dialogue between two friends. Write about 60 words. Use these ideas to help you.**

- one friend is bored
- the other friend suggests something to do
- the first friend doesn't like the idea very much
- the second friend suggests another thing to do (go for a walk, go to the movies, play video games, etc.)

9 WHO'S HUNGRY?

Grammar rap!

GRAMMAR

must / mustn't

→ SB p.86

1 ★☆☆ Complete the sentences with *must* or *mustn't*.

My very healthy mom says:

0 I *mustn't* drink too much soda.
1 I ______ eat more vegetables.
2 I ______ eat snacks or chocolate before meals.
3 I ______ go to bed late.
4 I ______ play sports after school.
5 I ______ drink more water.

2 ★☆☆ Circle the correct options.

0 A Dad, do we have any fruit?
B No, we don't. I (*must*) / *mustn't* buy some.

1 A Do you want to come to my house after school?
B I can't. I've got a clarinet lesson tomorrow so I *must* / *mustn't* practice tonight.

2 A What day is it today?
B It's Wednesday. We have PE this morning. You *must* / *mustn't* forget your PE clothes.

3 A What a cute hamster! Can we take it home?
B OK, but you *must* / *mustn't* take care of it.

4 A I'm not ready yet.
B Hurry up then. We *must* / *mustn't* miss the bus.

5 A I'm ready, Mom.
B Good. The movie starts in an hour, and we *must* / *mustn't* be late.

6 A Hey Dad, can I have one of these apples?
B Yes, but you *must* / *mustn't* wash it before you eat it.

3 ★★★ Complete the sentences with *must* (✓) or *mustn't* (✗) and a verb from the list.

be | buy | eat | finish | forget | give | remember | wash | ~~write~~

0 Ellie *must write* an email to her friend Maria in Colombia. (✓)
1 Marcus ______ home late today. (✗)
2 Helena ______ to take her tablet to school. (✓)
3 Oscar and Joao ______ to clean their bedrooms. (✗)
4 Dario ______ the book back to Jose. (✓)
5 Frida and Sofia ______ a present for their friend Jana. (✓)
6 Mateo ______ his homework before dinner. (✓)
7 We ______ any food in the classroom. (✗)
8 We ______ our hands before we eat lunch. (✓)

4 ★★★ Write five things you *must* or *mustn't* do this year.

0 *I must learn a lot of new English words.*
1 ______
2 ______
3 ______
4 ______
5 ______

can (asking for permission)

→ SB p.87

5 ★★☆ Put the words in order to make questions.

0 we / Can / the hockey game / Saturday / on / go / to / ?
Can we go to the hockey game on Saturday?

1 have / I / Can / fries / dinner / for / ?
______

2 I / Can / invite / Toby / to / my birthday party / ?
______

3 go / we / Can / the park / to / school / after / ?
______

4 call / I / Can / my sister / ?
______

5 I / wear / Can / green / sweater / your / today / ?
______

6 ★★☆ **Match the children's questions with Dad's answers.**

0 *Can I take your laptop to school with me?* — d
1 *Can we go swimming on Sunday?*
2 *Can I go to Kate's house after school tonight?*
3 *Can Mike and I go climbing this weekend?*

a *No, we can't. The pool is closed this weekend.*
b *Yes, of course you can. But don't come home late.*
c *Well, OK. But be careful.*
d *No, you can't. I need it for work.*

I'd like ... / Would you like ...? → SB p.89

7 ★☆☆ **Write sentences using *'d like* / *Would ... like*.**

0 I / tomato soup
I'd like tomato soup.
1 my mom / steak salad
______
2 what / you / for dessert / ?
______
3 Dad / ice cream for dessert / ?
______

8 ★★☆ **Put the conversation in order.**

[ ] **Waiter** (*five minutes later*) Are you ready to order?
[ ] **Waiter** Four soups, OK. And what would you like for the main course?
[ ] **Waiter** And finally, any drinks?
[ ] **Waiter** OK, so would you like a starter?
[*1*] **Waiter** Good evening. Would you like a table for four?
[ ] **Customer** Yes, please.
[ ] **Customer** Yes, we are.
[ ] **Customer** Just water for everyone, thanks.
[ ] **Customer** We'd like one cheese salad, one steak with potatoes and vegetables, one pizza, and one burger and fries, please.
[ ] **Customer** Yes, please. We'd like two tomato soups and two vegetable soups.

PRONUNCIATION
Intonation – giving two choices
Go to page 121.

9 ★★☆ **Look at the menu on page 88 of the Student's Book and complete the conversation so it is true for you.**

Waiter Are you ready to order?
You Yes, I am.
Waiter Would you like a starter?
You ______
Waiter And what would you like for the main course?
You ______
Waiter And would you like a dessert?
You ______
Waiter Any drinks?
You Yes, ______

GET IT RIGHT!

like and *would like*

We use *like* to say that something is nice.
✓ *I like ice cream. It's delicious!*
We use *would like* to ask for something we want or to ask somebody what they want.
✓ *I would like a burger, please.*
✗ *~~I like~~ a burger, please.*
✓ *Would you like a burger?*
✗ *~~You like~~ a burger?*
Circle the correct options.
0 I *like* / *(would like)* to come to your house tomorrow.
1 I *like* / *would like* a VR headset for my birthday.
2 I *like* / *would like* this house, and I'm happy living here.
3 I *like* / *would like* traveling to different countries.
4 I *like* / *would like* to go shopping on Monday.
5 I'm thirsty. I *like* / *would like* a drink of water.
6 When I have time, I *like* / *would like* cooking.

VOCABULARY
Food and drinks

SB p.86

1 ★☆☆ **Look at the pictures and complete the crossword. What's the mystery sentence?**

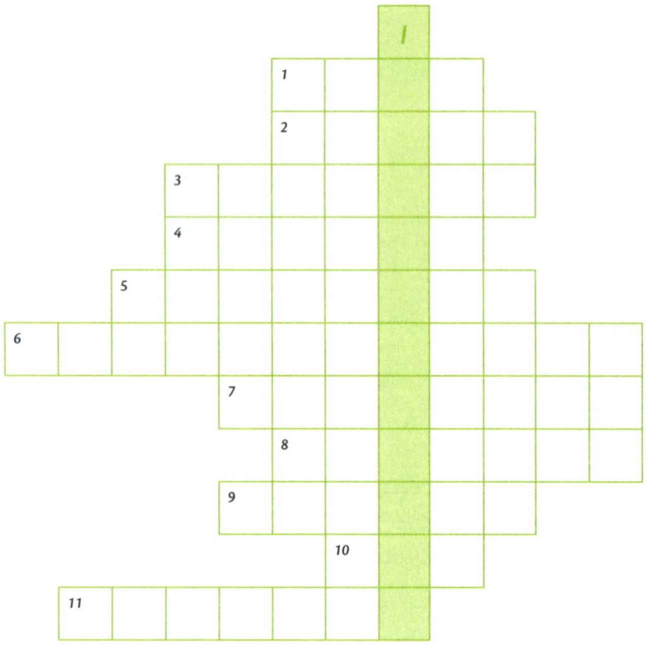

The mystery sentence is: ______________________

2 ★★☆ **Put the letters in order to make food words.**

0 We're having ___*beef*___ with potatoes and vegetables for lunch today. (e b e f)
1 My mom doesn't like __________ . (b l a m)
2 I often drink __________ with my breakfast. (l i m k)
3 I sometimes have an __________ after dinner. (p l p a e)
4 I'd like __________ and ice cream for dessert. (s t a r w b i r r e e s)
5 I like most vegetables, but I don't like __________ . (a c o r r t s)

Meals

SB p.89

3 ★☆☆ **Find and circle nine breakfast items in the word snake.**

abreadonbutterilkhoneymotoastljamogeggnyogurtatcerealetfruitth

4 ★★☆ **Put the words in order to make sentences or questions.**

0 you / do / usually / eat / for / breakfast, / What / Dora / ?
What do you usually eat for breakfast, Dora?
1 always / I / eat / an / egg / breakfast / for / .
____
2 usually / I / eat / toast / .
____
3 you / lunch / usually / have / for / What / do / ?
____
4 often / I / have / baked potato / a / .
____
5 sometimes / have / I / steak / vegetables / with / .
____
6 do / you / What / usually / drink / meals, / with / your / Dora / ?
____
7 drink / I / usually / or water / fruit juice / .
____

5 ★★☆ **Check (✓) the things Dora has for breakfast and lunch in Exercise 4.**

☐ fruit	☐ pizza	☐ yogurt
☐ toast	☐ spaghetti	☐ cereal
☐ an egg	☐ vegetables	☐ steak
☐ water	☐ baked potato	☐ chicken
☐ coffee	☐ fruit juice	☐ fries

6 ★★★ **Write sentences about Luca and Jamie using the words in parentheses.**

	always	often	sometimes	never
breakfast	an egg	toast	cereal	yogurt
lunch	coffee	a sandwich	pizza	soup
dinner	soup	pasta	fish	salad

0 *They sometimes have cereal for breakfast.* (sometimes)
1 ______________________ (always)
2 ______________________ (often)
3 ______________________ (never)
4 ______________________ (sometimes)
5 ______________________ (often)

REFERENCE

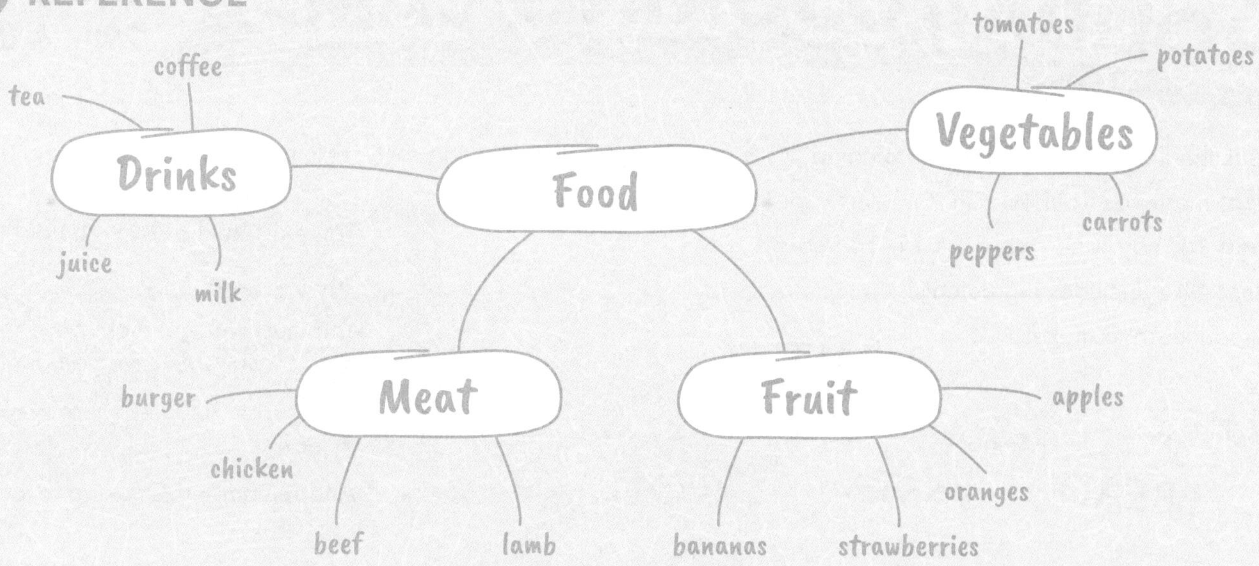

VOCABULARY *EXTRA*

1 **Write the name of each food under the photos. Use words from the photos.**

cheese | garlic | grapes | lemon | melon | onion | sour cream

1 ____________

2 ____________

3 ____________

4 ____________

5 ____________

6 ____________

7 ____________

2 **Put the food from Exercise 1 into the correct category in the table.**

dairy	fruit	vegetables
milk	*apple*	*carrot*

Mid-term

HOLIDAY COOKING CAMP

October 28th, 29th, & 30th

This is the third year of our cooking camp. It's a great way to start cooking for yourself!

Time: mornings from 10 a.m. to 1 p.m., for three days

Open to: boys and girls ages 11–14 years

Price: $45 (includes ingredients)

You can learn to make:

CAKES PIZZA HEALTHY SOUPS FRUIT SMOOTHIES BREAD PASTA

- ★ You must be 11–14 years old.
- ★ You must love food.
- ★ You must wear a chef's hat (don't worry, we give you one!).
- ★ You mustn't be late. There's a lot to learn.
- ★ And remember! Cooking is fun!

Your teacher Marianne is an excellent cook, and she loves good food. She has family from Spain, Turkey, Italy, and Russia. Marianne loves and cooks food from all of those countries. Come and learn to cook with her.

Our cooking camps are very popular, so sign up now!! Call 212-231-6564 to reserve your place.

READING

1 Read the leaflet for Cooking camp. What can you learn to make? Check (✓) the correct photos.

A

B

C

D

E

2 Read the leaflet again and correct the sentences.

0 Cooking camp is in November.
Cooking camp is in October.

1 Cooking camp is for three afternoons.
______

2 You don't make any drinks.
______

3 Marianne has family from Germany.
______

4 You must be 8–11 years old.
______

5 You mustn't wear any special clothes.
______

6 You mustn't be on time.
______

7 Remember that cooking is important.
______

3 CRITICAL THINKING **Answer the questions about the food camp.**

1 What things on the list are healthy things to cook?

2 Can you think of one reason why cooking is fun?

3 Think of two reasons why it is important for young people to learn to cook.

4 Complete the questionnaire for the Cooking camp so it is true for you.

COOKING CAMP
Questionnaire

1 What's your name? ______

2 How old are you? ______

3 What is your favorite dish? ______

4 Do you help your parents in the kitchen? ______

5 Can you cook? ______

6 What can you cook? ______

DEVELOPING Writing

My birthday meal plan

1 INPUT **Read the text about Sam's birthday dinner. What does he never drink on his birthday?**

My family usually eats healthy food, like rice and meat with vegetables and fruit for dessert. But on my birthday, we always have a special dinner together. We sometimes have my mom's amazing pizza, and sometimes chicken with hot sauce, fries, and salad (my favorite!). For dessert, we have my favorite ice cream – strawberry. My mom always makes my birthday cake. It's usually chocolate cake. I never drink soda on my birthday. I like lemonade.

2 ANALYZE **Answer the questions.**

0 How often does Sam's family eat healthy food?
They usually eat healthy food.

1 What is his favorite birthday meal?
____

2 What does he have for dessert on his birthday?
____

3 What does his mother always make him?
____

4 What does he usually drink on his birthday?
____

3 PLAN **Think about a dinner your family often eats on normal days. Now plan a special birthday meal with your favorite foods. Write your food choices in the table. Use words from the list and your own ideas.**

baked potato | bread | burger | chicken
chocolate | chocolate cake | eggs | fish
fries | fruit | fruit juice | ice cream
meat | milk | pasta | pizza | rice | salad
soda | soup | toast | vegetables | water

	normal meal	special birthday meal
food and drink		

4 PRODUCE **Use your notes from Exercise 3 to write a birthday meal plan. Use the text in Exercise 1 to help you. Write about 60 words.**

WRITING TIP: Adding detail

Add more detail to your writing by using adverbs of frequency:

- How often do you eat things?

You can answer this question with *always*, *usually*, *sometimes*, and *never*.

I sometimes have my mom's pizza.
I never drink soda.
I usually have fruit for dessert.
I always have a special birthday lunch with my family.

LISTENING

1 9.02 **Listen and check (✓) the things on the menu that the family decides to order.**

The BURGER and SALAD BAR

MENU

STARTERS

Soup of the day* ☐

Salad bar ☐

MAIN COURSE

Our delicious **burgers**!

★ Beef ☐ ★ Lamb ☐ ★ Vegetable ☐

Options from the grill!

★ Chicken ☐ ★ Steak ☐ ★ Fish ☐

SIDES

Fries ☐

Baked potato ☐

Vegetables of the day* ☐

Onion rings ☐

DRINKS

Lemonade ☐

Soda ☐

Apple juice ☐

Orange juice ☐

Hot tea ☐

Coffee ☐

Water ☐

DESSERT

Chef's dessert of the day* ☐

Carrot cake ☐

Ice cream:

★ Strawberry ☐ ★ Chocolate ☐ ★ Vanilla ☐

** Look at the board on the wall!*

2 9.02 **Listen again and mark the sentences T (true) or F (false).**

0 You choose your own food at the salad bar. *T*
1 The soup of the day is tomato. ☐
2 Jason loves broccoli and carrots. ☐
3 Jason orders three things. ☐
4 Dad doesn't want a starter. ☐
5 Ashley has a small dessert. ☐

DIALOGUE

3 **Circle the correct options.**

Waiter Are you ready to [0]*sit down* / *order*?
Customer 1 Yes, we are.
Waiter Would you like a [1]*starter* / *main course*?
Customer 1 Yes, please. I'd like tomato soup.
Customer 2 And I'd like vegetable soup.
Waiter And what would you like for the [2]*dessert* / *main course*?
Customer 1 I'd like chicken salad, please.
Customer 2 And I'd like fish and a baked potato, please.
Waiter And for [3]*starter* / *dessert*?
Customer 1 We'd like the chocolate cake, please.
Waiter Any [4]*drinks* / *desserts*?
Customer 1 Yes, please. I'd like apple juice.
Customer 2 And I'd like water.

PHRASES FOR FLUENCY → SB p.90

4 **Complete the conversations with phrases from the list.**

Of course. | Be careful! | a little | the thing is

Conversation 1

A Can you take these plates to the table?
B OK.
A ________________ Don't drop them.
B It's OK, Dad. Don't worry!

Conversation 2

A What's for dinner?
B It's pizza.
A Oh, no.
B What's wrong with pizza? I love it.
A Well, ________________, I don't like tomatoes.

Conversation 3

A Is there any cheese on the baked potato?
B Yes, there is, and there's ________________ butter, too.

Conversation 4

A Would you like some vegetables with your steak?
B ________________ I love vegetables.

SUM IT UP

1 Put the letters in order to find the food words.

What's on Mario's pizza?

0 seeche *cheese*
1 repspep ________
2 kicench ________
3 oestomta ________

What would Evalina like for dinner?

4 keast ________
5 topoesta ________
6 dasal ________

What's in Emma's dessert?

7 cochlateo ________
8 cierecam ________
9 rawsterriebs ________
10 nabana ________

CAFÉ ________	
starters ________ ________	*drinks* ________ ________
main courses ________ ________ ________ ________	*desserts* ________ ________ ________

2 Complete the menu. Use food and drink words from the unit.

- Think of a name for your café.
- Create a milkshake or a smoothie.
- Make a special pizza for your café.
- Create meals with the food words.
- Create one unusual meal.

For example: *Strawberry and Orange Salad* or *Carrot and Orange Soup*

3 Imagine you have a customer at your café. Complete the conversation.

Waiter Hello and welcome to Café [1]________ .
Customer 1 Hello. We'd like a table for two.
Waiter OK. Follow me, please.
(5 minutes later)
Waiter Are you ready to order now?
Customer 1 Yes, we are.
Waiter Would you like a starter?
Customer 1 Yes, please. [2]________ and my friend [3]________ .
Waiter And what [4]________ for the main course?
Customer 1 [5]________ , please.
Customer 2 And [6]________ .
Waiter And for dessert?
Customer 1 [7]________ , please.
Customer 2 And [8]________ .
Waiter Any drinks?
Customer 1 Yes, please. [9]________ , and my friend [10]________ .

10 BIG SUCCESSES

Grammar rap!

GRAMMAR

Simple past: *was / wasn't; were / weren't; there was / were*

→ SB p.94

1 ★☆☆ Circle the correct options.

0 You *was* / (*were*) late.
1 It *wasn't* / *weren't* his book.
2 I *was* / *were* at home yesterday.
3 We *was* / *were* at the movies.
4 They *wasn't* / *weren't* at the hockey game last night.
5 She *was* / *were* my best friend.

2 ★★☆ Complete the sentences with *was, were, wasn't,* or *weren't*.

0 I ___*was*___ (✓) born in Mexico City.
1 My grandma __________ (✗) a pilot.
2 Adam and Jay __________ (✓) in the park yesterday.
3 We __________ (✗) at my aunt's house last night.
4 Leon __________ (✗) at the basketball court on Sunday.
5 It __________ (✓) my birthday yesterday.

3 ★★★ Complete the text with the correct simple past form of *to be*.

The Montgolfier brothers [0] ___*were*___ the inventors of the hot-air balloon. They [1] __________ (✓) French. Their names [2] __________ (✓) Joseph-Michel and Jacques-Étienne. Joseph-Michel [3] __________ (✓) born in 1740, and Jacques-Étienne [4] __________ (✓) born in 1745. There [5] __________ (✓) sixteen children in the family. Their father [6] __________ (✗) an inventor. He [7] __________ (✓) a paper manufacturer. The first balloon flight [8] __________ (✓) in June of 1783. There [9] __________ (✗) any passengers. There [10] __________ (✓) no one on the balloon. The second flight [11] __________ (✓) in Paris in September of 1783. This time, there [12] __________ (✓) three passengers, but the passengers [13] __________ (✗) people. They [14] __________ (✓) a chicken, a duck, and a sheep.

Simple past: *Was he ...? / Were you ...?*

→ SB p.95

4 ★☆☆ Match the questions with the answers.

0 Were you born in Rome? — e
1 Was your grandfather a chef?
2 Was Valentina an astronaut?
3 Was it your phone?
4 Was I late to the party?
5 Were you and I on time?
6 Were Sandra and Joel at the youth club yesterday?

a No, he wasn't.
b Yes, you were!
c Yes, it was.
d No, we weren't.
e Yes, I was.
f No, they weren't.
g Yes, she was.

5 ★★★ Put the words in order to make questions. Then look at the text in Exercise 3 and answer the questions.

0 Were / the / inventors / brothers / Montgolfier / ?
Were the Montgolfier brothers inventors?
Yes, they were.

1 they / Italian / Were / ?
____
____

2 Was / Joseph-Michel / in 1740 / born / ?
____
____

3 Was / inventor / an / their / father / ?
____
____

4 the / Was / in / flight / first / June of 1795 / ?
____
____

5 flight / second / Prague / in / Was / the / ?
____
____

6 Were / there / passengers / any / ?
____
____

Simple past: regular verbs

SB p.97

6 ★☆☆ **Complete the table with the correct simple past of the verbs in the list.**

believe | carry | cry | ~~finish~~
help | like | live | study | work

+ -ed	+ -d	+ -ied
finished		

7 ★★☆ **Put the words in order to make sentences. Put the verbs in the simple past.**

0 uncle / My / study / college / in / medicine / .
My uncle studied medicine in college.

1 finish / degree / his / He / 2010 / in / .
______

2 at / hospital / a / He / work / Denver / in / .
______

3 in / He / San Francisco / three / years / for / live / .
______

4 like / He / California / very / much / .
______

5 move / He / Los Angeles / to / 2014 / in / .
______

8 ★★☆ **Complete the text with the simple past form of the verbs in parentheses.**

DAVID ATTENBOROUGH

The famous scientist David Attenborough [0] *lived* (live) in London as a child. He [1]______ (study) at Cambridge University and later in London. In 1950, Attenborough [2]______ (marry) Jane Oriel, and they had two children. He [3]______ (work) for the BBC for many years as a producer, but he [4]______ (want) to make shows about nature. In 1972, he [5]______ (stop) working at the BBC and [6]______ (start) to make nature shows. He soon [7]______ (return) to the BBC and made many famous series, including *Life on Earth* in 1976, with 96 episodes! Over many years, Attenborough and his teams [8]______ (discover) new ways to film animals and plants. He [9]______ (travel) to all seven continents, and millions of people [10]______ (watch) his programs.

9 ★★★ **Complete the text with the simple past form of the verbs in parentheses.**

Florence Nightingale

Florence Nightingale [0] *was* (be) a famous English nurse. She [1]______ (be) born in Florence, Italy, in 1820. Later, her parents [2]______ (move) back to England. As a child, she [3]______ (like) helping others. She [4]______ (care) for sick people and animals. She [5]______ (want) to be a nurse.

In 1851, she [6]______ (work) as a nurse in Germany. In 1853, there [7]______ (be) a war. It [8]______ (be) called the Crimean War. They [9]______ (need) nurses, so Florence [10]______ (sail) with nurses to help. They [11]______ (help) the British soldiers there. Life [12]______ (not be) easy. The war [13]______ (end) in 1856. Florence Nightingale [14]______ (return) to England as a hero. She [15]______ (die) in London in 1910.

PRONUNCIATION
Simple past regular verbs Go to page 121.

GET IT RIGHT!

was / wasn't* and *were / weren't

We use *was, wasn't, were,* and *weren't* to talk about the past. We use *am, am not, is, isn't, are,* and *aren't* to talk about now.

✓ *Yesterday was my birthday.*

✗ *Yesterday is my birthday.*

Correct the sentences.

0 Geoff isn't at school yesterday.
Geoff wasn't at school yesterday.

1 There is a great movie on TV last night.
______

2 Hello! I was very happy to see you.
______

3 All my friends are there for my birthday last night.
______

4 Is Laura with you yesterday evening?
______

5 Gigi was worried about her exam today.
______

6 They aren't late for school yesterday.
______

VOCABULARY

Time expressions: past

SB p.94

1 ★☆☆ Complete the table with the words from the list.

afternoon | evening | ~~month~~
morning | night | Saturday
3 o'clock | year | 6 p.m.
10:30 | 1969 | 2015

last	in
month	
at	**yesterday**

2 ★☆☆ Complete the dialogues with *at, in, last,* and *yesterday*.

0 **A** Where were you *last* night?
B I was at home.

1 **A** Were you at school ____________ afternoon?
B Yes, I was.

2 **A** Was Jaime at the party ____________ Saturday?
B No, he was at home.

3 **A** Was your dad born ____________ 1980?
B No, he wasn't.

4 **A** Was Tim still at school ____________ 5 p.m. this evening?
B Yes, he was.

3 ★★☆ Where were you? Write sentences with *at, last,* and *yesterday* and the time if necessary.

0 (at) *I was on the bus at 8 o'clock.*

1 (at) ____________

2 (last) ____________

3 (yesterday) ____________

The weather

SB p.97

4 ★★☆ Complete the sentences and the crossword with the same words.

ACROSS

4 Today it's ____________, so we don't need our sunglasses.
5 It's ____________, so don't forget your umbrella.
7 It's ____________, so it's a great day to fly your kite.
8 It's ____________ – there are a lot of people on the beach today.

DOWN

1 Today is beautiful and ____________. Let's sit outside.
2 Drink a lot of water today – it's very ____________!
3 You can make a snowman today. It's ____________.
4 It's ____________ today, so don't forget to wear warm clothes.

5 ★★☆ Circle the correct options in these phone conversations.

1 **A** What's the weather like?
B It's [0]*(sunny)* / *cloudy*. I'm wearing sunglasses.
A Is it [1]*cold* / *hot*?
B Yes, it is. I'm wearing a T-shirt. What's the weather like there?
A It's very [2]*cloudy* / *windy* here. Listen. Can you hear it?
B Yes, I can.

2 **A** What's the weather like?
B It's [3]*raining* / *cloudy*. I can't play soccer outside today.
A Is it [4]*cold* / *hot*?
B Yes, it is. I'm wearing a sweater and a coat. What's the weather like there?
A It's [5]*snowing* / *windy* here. We can't go to school today because we can't get out of the house.
B Really?

6 ★★★ Write sentences about the weather today. What can or can't you do?

____

____

____

____

REFERENCE

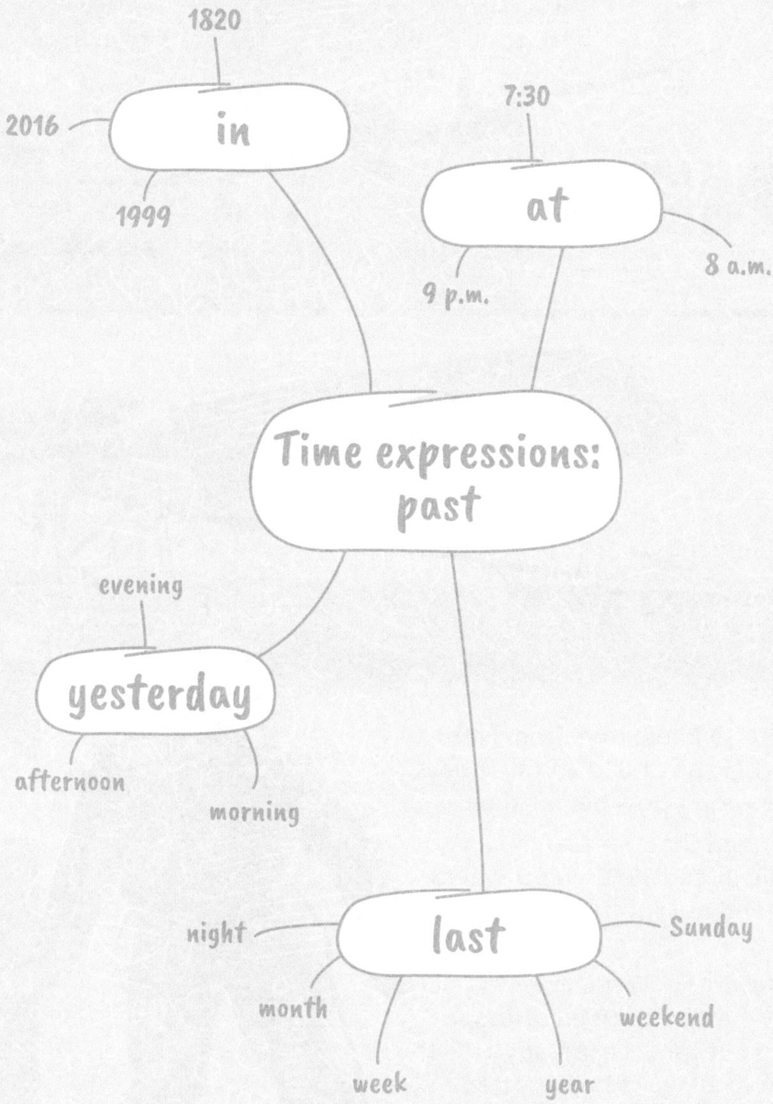

The weather

It's sunny.

It's cloudy.

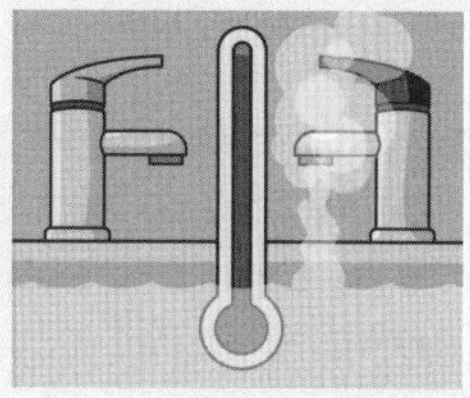
It's hot.

It's raining.

It's snowing.

It's windy.

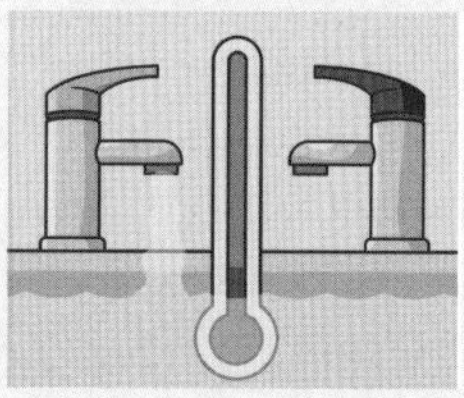
It's cold.

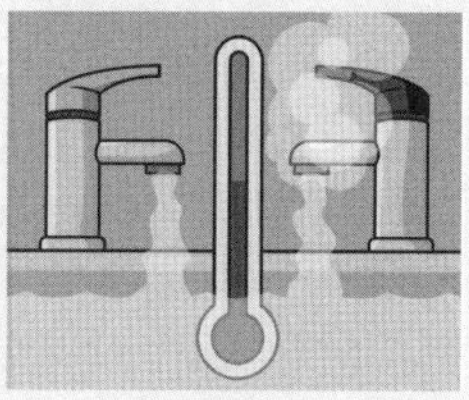
It's warm.

VOCABULARY *EXTRA*

1 **Match the definitions with the words from the list.**

after | ~~at noon~~ | at midnight | before | early | late

0 in the middle of the day: *at noon*
1 before something starts: ___________
2 earlier than something else: ___________
3 after something starts: ___________
4 at 12 o'clock at night: ___________
5 in the time following something else: ___________

2 **Put the letters in order to make words.**

0 Please don't be *late* for the movie. We mustn't miss the beginning! (a l t e)
1 My little sister's birthday in June is ___________ my birthday in May. (t e f a r)
2 Can you come ___________ the party starts to help me with the food? (e o e r f b)
3 The music festival starts ___________ on Saturday. (t a o n o n)
4 To get a good seat at the concert, you need to arrive very ___________ (e y l r a)
5 The last bus home from the city center is ___________ (t a d g h i i m n t)

Flying MACHINES

A

Do you like flying? Did you know that there are different ways to explore the skies? Here we look at two incredible flying inventions from France!

B

On July 25, 1909, the French aviator Louis Blériot flew a monoplane (a plane with one pair of wings) across the English Channel - the sea between France and England. He developed the first monoplane with a pilot, and he was the first person to fly from one country to another across the sea! The plane didn't look very strong, but it only took 36 minutes and 30 seconds to fly the 35 kilometers from France to England. An English newspaper gave him a prize of £1,000. In those days, most people only dreamed of flying, because it wasn't possible for them.

The invention of the jet plane in the 1930s changed that. Jet planes can go very fast, very far, and carry hundreds of people. By the 1960s, air travel as we know today became possible. Now people, and not just rich people, fly all over the world.

And inventors are still finding new ways to fly! Another Frenchman, Franky Zapata, was a jet ski World Champion. When he stopped racing, he invented a hoverboard called the Flyboard Air. It uses technology similar to drones, and jet plane fuel. On August 4, 2019, 110 years after Blériot, Zapata crossed the Channel on his Flyboard Air, at a top speed of 170 kilometers an hour, and arrived safely on the south coast of England in 22 minutes. He looked like a superhero in a comic!

Can you imagine people on hoverboards flying everywhere in the future? Who knows! In 1909, no one imagined people flying away on vacation! How quickly things change!

C

READING

1 **Read the article about flying machines. Put the photos in order from old to new (1–3).**

2 **Read the article again. What do these numbers mean?**

0 2019 *Franky Zapata crossed the Channel on the Flyboard Air.*
1 35 ______
2 1909 ______
3 22 ______
4 1,000 ______
5 170 ______

3 CRITICAL THINKING **Read the article again and check (✓) the words you think describe Zapata's hoverboard. Why did you choose each word? Write your reasons.**

- fun ☐
- expensive ☐
- dangerous ☐
- climate-friendly ☐
- easy to use ☐
- a great idea ☐

______
______
______
______

DEVELOPING Writing

A short biography

1 INPUT Read the fact file and biography of Alicia Keys. Where was she born?

A Personal details

Alicia Keys is an American singer, pianist, and songwriter. Her real name is Alicia Augello-Cook. She was born in New York on January 25, 1981, and lived in a poor area. She is married to a DJ, Swizz Beatz, and they have two sons.

B Professional

Alicia went to the Professional Performing Arts School in New York and studied classical piano. A record company gave her a contract when she was only 15. She has many hit songs and successful albums.

C Charity work

Alicia helped start a charity in Africa called Keep a Child Alive, which helps sick children, and she organizes concerts to raise money every year. She also tries to help fight racism and poverty.

FACT FILE

Alicia Keys

1 Date of birth: January 25, 1981
2 Nationality: American
3 Education: Professional Performing Arts School, New York
4 Real name: Alicia Augello-Cook
5 Family: married to DJ Swizz Beatz, two sons
6 Place of birth: New York
7 Job: singer, musician, songwriter
8 Big break: Record contract in 1996, age 15
9 Charity work: Keep a Child Alive (charity in Africa, helps sick children)

2 ANALYZE Match sections 1–9 in the fact file with paragraphs A–C.

Paragraph A: Section(s): ____________

Paragraph B: Section(s): ____________

Paragraph C: Section(s): ____________

3 Read paragraphs A and B again and find three facts that are not in the fact file. Then match them with the correct sections in the fact file.

4 PLAN Use the information in the list to complete the fact file about Millie Bobby Brown.

actress, producer | British | ~~Millie Bobby Brown~~
2016, Eleven in *Stranger Things*, age 12
Marbella, Spain (now lives in the US)
Millie Bobby Brown | February 19, 2004
two sisters, one brother
UNICEF ambassador (youngest ever)

FACT FILE

Millie Bobby Brown

1 Nationality:
2 Place of birth:
3 Date of birth:
4 Real name:
5 Family:
6 Job:
7 Big break:
8 Charity work:

WRITING TIP: Organization

A biography includes a lot of information, so it needs good organization.
One way to do this is with paragraphs and headings, like in the text about Alicia Keys:

- A Personal details
- B Professional
- C Charity work

5 PRODUCE Use the fact file to write a short biography of Millie Bobby Brown. You can use the internet to find more information. Write about 70 words.

LISTENING

1 Look at the picture and guess the answers to the questions.

1 Who is the man in the photo?

____

2 What did he write about?

____

2 10.02 **Listen to Tom talking about a writer. Circle the correct options.**

0 Tom's hero was a *writer* / *artist*.
1 His most famous book was *Narnia* / *The Jungle Book*.
2 His parents were *English* / *Indian*.
3 His father was *a doctor* / *an artist*.
4 Rudyard Kipling *loved* / *hated* India.
5 He was *happy* / *unhappy* with the Holloways.
6 He *loved* / *hated* books.
7 He was *happy* / *unhappy* at school in Devon.
8 After school he lived in *Italy* / *India*.
9 He worked for a *newspaper* / *university*.

3 10.02 **Listen again and complete the text with the correct words.**

Rudyard Kipling's parents were English. They [0] *moved* to India. His father was an artist, and he worked at a school of Art in Bombay (which is now called Mumbai). Kipling loved India. He loved the [1] __________ and the culture. However, he didn't have a happy childhood. His parents wanted him to go to [2] __________ in England. When he was six years old, he lived with a [3] __________ , the Holloways, in a seaside [4] __________ in England. Mrs. Holloway was very bad to him. He [5] __________ life there, and he was very unhappy. Luckily, he [6] __________ books. He loved books. They [7] __________ him from his unhappy life.

DIALOGUE

4 Complete the conversation with the past simple of the verbs in parentheses. Then put the conversation in order.

[1] **Ben** [0] *Were* (be) you at home yesterday?
[ ] **Ben** Did they? [1] __________ (be) they good?
[ ] **Ben** [2] __________ (be) it a good party?
[ ] **Ben** Oh, I remember. It [3] __________ (be) your cousin's birthday yesterday, right?
[ ] **Sam** Yes, they [4] __________ (be) very good.
[ ] **Sam** Yes, it [5] __________ (be). I loved it.
[ ] **Sam** Yes, it [6] __________ (be). Her brothers are in a band. They [7] __________ (play) at her party.
[ ] **Sam** No, I [8] __________ (not be). I [9] __________ (be) at my cousin's house.

Train to THINK

Sequencing

5 Complete the sequence with words from the list.

And then | Finally | First

> __________ > Then > __________
> After that > __________

6 Order the events in Rudyard Kipling's life. Then complete the sentences with sequencing words from Exercise 5.

Rudyard Kipling (1865–1936)

[ ] __________ , he died in London in 1936.
[ ] __________ he lived in a seaside town in England with the Holloway family.
[ ] *First* , Rudyard Kipling lived in India.
[ ] __________ he moved to a school in Devon.
[ ] __________ , he moved back to India, and he worked for a newspaper.

EXAM SKILLS: LISTENING

Listening for key words

1 10.03 **Listen and tick (✓) the months you hear.**

January ☐ | February ☐ | March ☐ | April ☐ | May ☐ | June ☐ | July ☐
August ☐ | September ☐ | October ☐ | November ☐ | December ☐

LISTENING TIP

- First, learn to listen for key words, for example, the months of the year.
- Next, you need to complete the profile. Listen carefully for the dates, the jobs and the places.

Remember! You don't need to understand everything.

2 10.04 **Listen and circle the correct options to complete Claude Monet's profile.**

Claude Monet

0 Job
writer / *painter*

1 Nationality
French / *Italian*

2 Born
14th *September* / *November* 1840

3 Mother's job
singer / *actor*

4 Father's job
gardener / *grocer*

5 September 1870
He lived in *London* / *New York*.

6 May 1871
He moved to *Germany* / *Holland*.

7 May 1883
He moved to Giverny in *France* / *Belgium*.

8 Died
5th *June* / *December* 1926

3 10.05 **Listen and complete Vincent Van Gogh's profile.**

Vincent Van Gogh

0 Job
painter

1 Nationality
______

2 Born
______

3 Studied
______

4 Moved to Paris
______

5 Lived with
______

6 Number of paintings sold when alive
______

7 Age died
______

8 Date died
______

9 Famous painting name
______

CONSOLIDATION

LISTENING

1 10.06 **Listen to Charlotte and Jack and circle the correct answers (A, B, or C).**

1 For breakfast, Charlotte doesn't want …
   A orange juice.
   B cereal.
   C eggs.
2 Charlotte arrived home at …
   A eleven o'clock.
   B twelve o'clock.
   C one o'clock.
3 Charlotte wants to read her …
   A emails.
   B newspaper.
   C tablet.

2 10.06 **Listen again. Mark the sentences T (true) or F (false).**

1 Charlotte wants yogurt for breakfast. ☐
2 She wants tea. ☐
3 Last night, Charlotte was at a party. ☐
4 Jack worked for five hours last night. ☐
5 Jack says he always works hard. ☐
6 The weather is rainy and cold. ☐
7 Charlotte wants to borrow Jack's tablet. ☐
8 Charlotte is going to work. ☐

GRAMMAR

3 **Circle the correct options.**

1 Dad, *can* / *must* I ask you a question?
2 Hurry up! We *must* / *mustn't* be late again.
3 Are you hungry? *Would* / *Do* you like some cake?
4 *It* / *There* wasn't a nice day yesterday. It was cold and rainy.
5 You really *can* / *must* be careful, John. Don't break it!
6 *Would* / *Do* you like this song?
7 *It* / *There* was a good basketball game on TV last night.
8 *I like* / *I'd like* a glass of water, please.
9 My brother *wasn't* / *weren't* at school yesterday.
10 I *study* / *studied* for the test last night.

4 **Complete the sentences with the correct form of verbs from the list.**

arrive | be (x2) | like | not be (x2) | rain
show | stay | travel | want | watch

Our vacation last year wasn't very good! We [1]__________ to Ohio by car. We [2]__________ very late, and the man at the hotel [3]__________ angry with us. Then he [4]__________ us the rooms. They [5]__________ really small and cold. We [6]__________ to change the rooms, but the man said that there [7]__________ any other rooms. We [8]__________ in the hotel for three nights. The weather [9]__________ good. It [10]__________ almost all the time! One day, I stayed in my room and [11]__________ TV for about six hours. But the food was good. We [12]__________ it a lot. Next year, we don't want to go to that hotel again.

VOCABULARY

5 **Complete the words.**

1 Do you want black coffee or coffee with m _ _ k?
2 It's cold and w _ _ _ y today.
3 I don't eat a lot of v _ _ _ _ _ _ _ _ s.
4 My favorite fruit is an o _ _ _ _ _ .
5 I was at home yesterday e _ _ _ _ _ g.
6 It was her birthday last M _ _ _ h.
7 There's no sun today – it's very c _ _ _ _ y.
8 I watched tennis yesterday a _ _ _ _ _ _ _ n.
9 I'd like apple juice and eggs for b _ _ _ _ _ _ _ t.
10 I love eating b _ _ _ _ s and fries.

6 **Complete the dialogue with words from the list.**

dinner | fruit | meat | night | ~~o'clock~~
potatoes | strawberries | tea

Liam What time do you usually eat in your family?
Nicky Well, we usually have lunch at one [0] *o'clock* . And then we have [1]__________ at eight in the evening.
Liam And what do you eat in the evening?
Nicky We have [2]__________ – beef or chicken – and some vegetables, like carrots or [3]__________ . I usually drink juice, but my parents like hot drinks, so they have [4]__________ .
Liam And then?
Nicky Then we have [5]__________ , usually apples, but last [6]__________ we had [7]__________ – they're my favorite!

DIALOGUE

7 10.07 **Complete the dialogue with the words from the list. There are two extra words. Then listen and check.**

bit | can | careful | course | liked | mustn't | thing | wanted | was | wasn't | were | weren't

Clara So, what was Jason's party like last night?

Giorgio It was great. We all enjoyed it. There [1]________________ great music, and I danced a lot. And all my friends were there.

Clara Was there any food?

Giorgio Yes. There [2]________________ sandwiches and cheese and some really nice chicken wings, too. The [3]________________ is …

Clara Yes?

Giorgio Well, Jason's mom cooked some risotto, and it [4]________________ good at all! No one [5] ________________ it. At the end of the party, it was all still there! I usually love risotto, but not that!

Clara Oh, dear. Oh, look. Jason's coming. Be [6]________________ ! We [7]________________ say anything about the risotto, OK?

Giorgio No, sure. Jason! Hi. How are you? Thanks for the party!

Jason Hi, Giorgio. Hi, Clara. No problem. I'm happy that you enjoyed it. But Giorgio, [8]________________ I ask you something?

Giorgio Uh, of [9]________________ . What?

Jason My mom's risotto. Was it really terrible? No one [10]________________ to eat it!

Clara Go on, Giorgio. I think you can tell him!

READING

8 Read Emily's email. Then correct the sentences.

1 Yesterday was Emily's fourteenth birthday.

____

2 The restaurant only serves Chinese food.

____

3 The restaurant was noisy.

____

4 Emily didn't like the soup.

____

5 Emily's mother and father don't eat fish.

____

6 Emily's family eat in restaurants a lot.

____

7 There was writing on the candles.

____

8 Emily's family is having dessert at a restaurant tonight.

____

Alli
Emily@thinkmail.com

Hi Alli,

Yesterday was my birthday, so my family had dinner in a restaurant in town. It's a Chinese restaurant, but they do all kinds of different foods there. There weren't a lot of other people in the restaurant, so it was very quiet.

The dinner was really nice. We started with vegetable soup – it was delicious! Then I ordered beef with peppers and mushrooms. My parents ordered fish (they don't eat meat) with vegetables and rice. And for dessert, I had banana and mango ice cream, my favorite! The food was great – I enjoyed my meal a lot. We don't usually eat in restaurants, so it was a special evening.

When we finished eating, a waiter came over with a big birthday cake! It had thirteen candles on it (of course!) and the words "Happy Birthday, Emily" in big letters in the middle. The waiters and my parents started to sing "Happy Birthday to You," and the other people in the restaurant joined in, too. At the end of the song, everyone clapped – it was really nice! There was enough cake for us and the other people in the restaurant, and there's some in the fridge in our kitchen now!

So, dessert at our house tonight is birthday cake!

Love,

Emily

WRITING

9 Write a paragraph about a good or bad meal you remember. Write about 60 words. Use the questions to help you.

- Where were you?
- What was the meal? (dinner? lunch?)
- Who was there?
- What was the food?
- Why was it a good/bad meal?

11 THE ANIMAL WORLD

Grammar rap!

GRAMMAR

Simple past: irregular verbs

→ SB p.104

1 ★☆☆ **Complete the table with the simple past or the base form of the verbs.**

base form	simple past
0 ran	*ran*
1	came
2	put
3 give	
4 see	
5	knew
6	drank
7 fall	
8 write	
9	took
10 eat	

2 ★★☆ **Complete the text with the simple past form of the verbs in parentheses.**

The Hill family's vacation

Last year, the Hill family from Utah decided to go on vacation in Arizona. They [0] *went* (go) to northern Arizona. Mr. Hill [1] __________ (make) a reservation at a hotel in Sedona. In Sedona, they [2] __________ (see) beautiful rock formations. Then Mandy [3] __________ (find) Out of Africa Wildlife Park on her computer. She [4] __________ (tell) her parents about the park with lions, zebras, and a lot of other animals. The website [5] __________ (say) the park had hundreds of animals. The whole family [6] __________ (think) it was a good idea to visit the park. So they [7] __________ (get) in the car and [8] __________ (drive) to the park. They [9] __________ (have) a really good time there!

Simple past (negative)

→ SB p.104

3 ★★★ **Write sentences about a birthday party. Use the simple past negative.**

0 my grandmother / to the party (come)
My grandmother didn't come to the party.

1 the band / classical music (play)
____

2 we / bread and butter (eat)
____

3 Adriana / me a dictionary (give)
____

4 Mom / my dress (make)
____

5 Rob / a spider on the table (see)
____

6 my father / us home (take)
____

7 Stefan / a snake in a box (find)
____

8 we / a movie (watch)
____

4 ★★☆ **Logan didn't have a good weekend. Complete the sentences with the simple past form of the verbs in the list.**

~~be~~ | be | decide | do | not do | not rain
not work | rain | try | use | want

0 Last weekend *was* awful.
1 It __________ all day on Saturday.
2 I __________ anything interesting.
3 I __________ to watch a movie, but the download __________ .
4 My brother __________ the computer for his homework all afternoon.
5 I __________ to go out, but it was too cold and wet.
6 But, it __________ on Sunday. Great!
7 So I __________ to ride my bike to the park.
8 But my bike __________ broken.
9 What __________ you __________ last weekend?

5 ★★★ Complete the text with the simple past form of a verb in the box.

eat | ~~go~~ | go | have | not be | not like
not want | not watch | see | share | spend | take

Sarah [0] *went* to Boston last weekend with three friends. They stayed in a student hotel. It was very cheap, but the rooms [1] ______________ very nice. Sarah [2] ______________ a room with Lisa. The hotel had a café, and on Friday evening, they [3] ______________ there because they were tired from the trip. But Craig and Alex [4] ______________ the pizza very much. On Saturday morning, Sarah and Alex [5] ______________ to the Museum of Natural History in Cambridge. They [6] ______________ a dodo and some dinosaurs. Craig and Lisa [7] ______________ to look at animals, so they [8] ______________ the morning in the Museum of Science instead. In the evening, they [9] ______________ the subway to the theater district, but they [10] ______________ a show because the tickets were very expensive. So they [11] ______________ burgers, and this time, the boys were happy!

Simple past (questions)

→ SB p.105

6 ★★★ Use the information in Exercise 5 and write questions about Sarah for these answers.

0 A *Where did Sarah go last weekend?*
B She went to Boston.

1 A Where ______________
B In a hotel.

2 A What ______________ on Friday?
B A pizza in the café.

3 A Where ______________
B In the Museum of Natural History.

4 A What ______________
B A dodo and some dinosaurs.

5 A What ______________
B A burger.

PRONUNCIATION
Short vowel sound /ʊ/ Go to page 121.

could / couldn't (ability)

→ SB p.107

7 ★★☆ Last year, Ben broke his leg, and they put it in a cast. What could he do? What couldn't he do? Use phrases from the list.

do his homework | eat a pizza | go swimming
listen to music | ~~play soccer~~ | play the guitar
ride a bike | text his friends | ~~watch TV~~

0 *Ben could watch TV.*
0 *He couldn't play soccer.*
1 He ______________
2 He ______________
3 He ______________
4 He ______________
5 He ______________
6 He ______________
7 He ______________

GET IT RIGHT!

Simple past

We always use the base form of the verb after *didn't* (in negative sentences) or *Did* (in questions).

✓ *I didn't go to the party last Saturday.*
✗ ~~*I didn't went to the party last Saturday.*~~
✓ *Did you visit the museum?*
✗ ~~*Did you visited the museum?*~~

Correct the sentences.

0 He didn't finished his homework.
He didn't finish his homework.

1 Jack didn't liked the party.
____

2 We didn't paid much for lunch at the zoo yesterday.
____

3 Did they enjoyed their vacation?
____

4 We didn't knew where it was, but finally we found it.
____

5 Billy's friend didn't ate a lot of food yesterday.
____

6 Did you went to the party?
____

VOCABULARY

Verb and noun pairs

→ SB p.104

1 ★★☆ Read the sentences. Are the underlined words correct (✓) or incorrect (✗)? Write the correct words.

0 I always <u>do</u> my homework. ✓

______

0 I <u>do</u> a shower every morning. ✗

take

1 I'm tired. Let's <u>take</u> a break now. ☐

______

2 We just <u>went</u> the shopping for the party. ☐

______

3 Try not to <u>do</u> a lot of mistakes. ☐

______

4 Please don't <u>make</u> too much noise when you come back. ☐

______

5 We <u>made</u> some great photos on vacation. ☐

______

6 Did you <u>do</u> a good time at the party? ☐

______

2 ★★☆ Complete the sentences with the correct verb in the correct form.

0 They ___*went*___ skiing last winter.

1 I always ______ excited the day before my birthday.

2 I always ______ something on the weekend. I never stay at home.

3 We live near an airport – the planes ______ a lot of noise every day.

4 Our weekend was fantastic! We ______ a party at our house.

5 Every day, when I wake up, I ______ a bath.

6 We weren't hungry so we didn't ______ breakfast.

7 ______ you always ______ the bus to school?

Adjectives

→ SB p.107

3 ★★☆ Put the letters in order to make adjectives. Then look at the pictures and write the phrases.

ovllye · marst · tydri · putdis · regnoudas · blehirro · gluy · teulauibf · tersniginet · lance

0 *a lovely gorilla* 1 ______ 2 ______ 3 ______ 4 ______ 5 ______ 6 ______ 7 ______ 8 ______ 9 ______

4 ★★☆ Complete the crossword and the sentences with the same words. What's the mystery word?

1 I don't like this movie; it's really ______ .

2 Snakes can sometimes be ______ .

3 Cats are very ______ animals.

4 I don't like that house. I think it's ______ .

5 I have to wash my parents' car because it's very ______ .

6 The class today was great. It was really ______ .

7 Some big cities aren't very ______ at night.

8 Hey! That was a really ______ thing to do!

9 Thank you for my ______ birthday present.

Mystery word: ______

REFERENCE

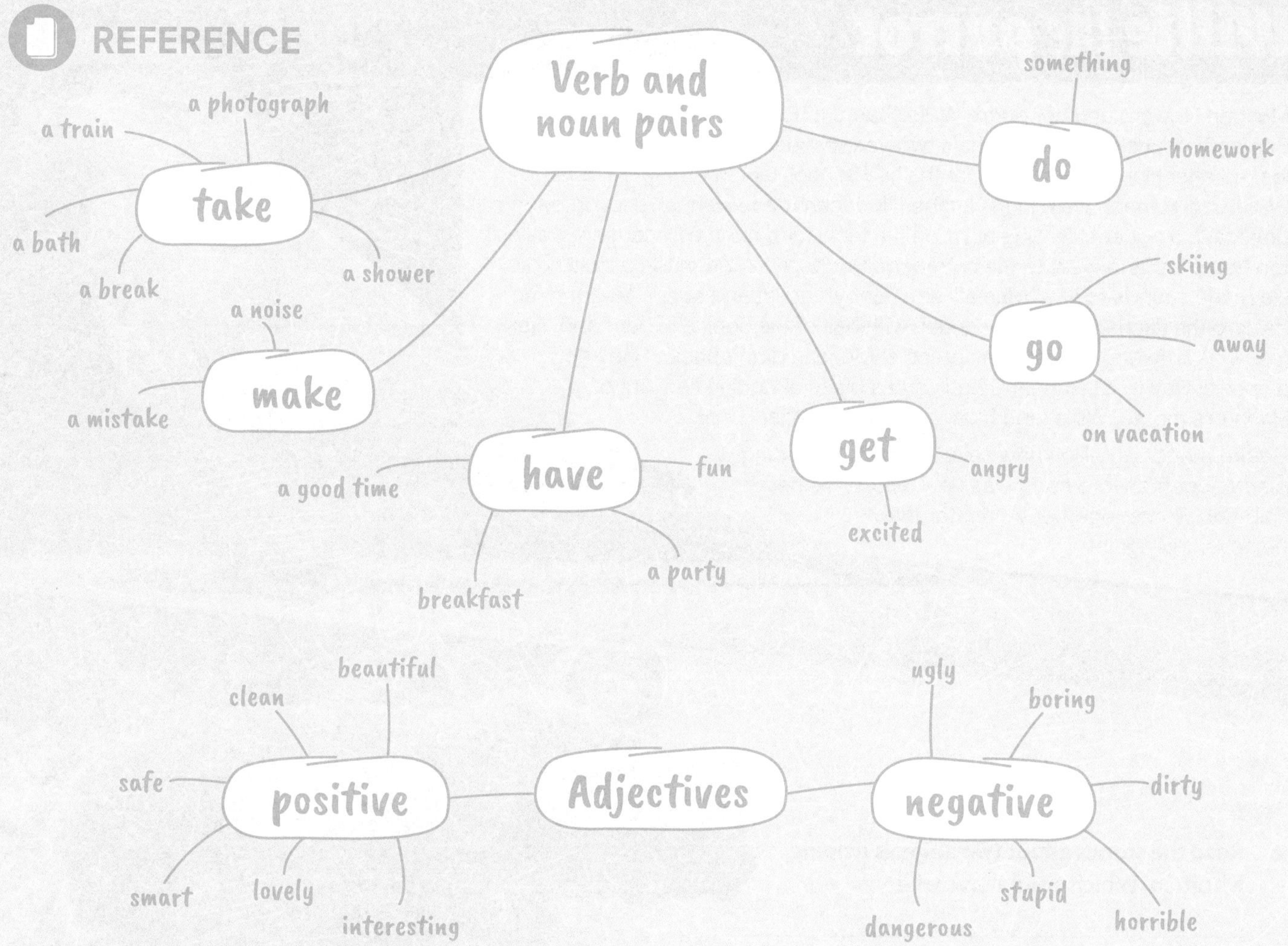

VOCABULARY *EXTRA*

1 Match the verb–noun combinations from the list with the definitions.

do nothing | get upset | go fishing | ~~go to bed~~ | have dinner | make friends

0 lie down to sleep *go to bed*
1 meet new people to hang out with ________
2 feel bad about something, like losing your phone ________
3 activity in a river or the ocean ________
4 eat in the evening ________
5 you sit in your room or on the sofa and relax ________

2 Complete the sentences using the past form of the verbs and nouns in Exercise 1.

0 At Ali's new school, everyone was friendly, and he *made friends* quickly.
1 Yesterday, I had a lot of homework, and I ________ at midnight!
2 Yesterday, they ________ at the new Italian restaurant.
3 Last Sunday, we stayed at home and ________ all day. It was really boring.
4 My mom and I ________ today. We caught lots to eat for dinner.
5 My parents ________ because my sister lost her free bus pass again.

Willie the parrot

Meagan Howard and her parrot Willie shared a house in Colorado with Samantha Kuusk and Samantha's two-year-old daughter, Hannah. Meagan looked after Hannah when Samantha had school. One morning, Meagan, Willie, and Hannah were in the kitchen. Meagan made Hannah's favorite breakfast, a hot cookie. She put it on the table for a minute because it was still too hot to eat and went to the bathroom. Suddenly, Willie made a loud noise. He made sounds to say "Mama!" and "Baby!" again and again. Meagan ran back to the kitchen and saw Hannah with half of the cookie in her hand. Her face was blue and she couldn't breathe! Meagan didn't panic. She knew a special way to hit Hannah's back and a piece of cookie flew out of Hannah's mouth. Willie (and Meagan) saved Hannah!

Before that day, Willie knew several words, including *mama*, but the word *baby* was new, and Willie never said two words together. And after that, he never did again!

READING

1 **Read the stories about two animals helping a human. Which animal was wild?**

____

2 **Read the sentences and underline the incorrect information. Then write correct sentences.**

Willie and the parrot

0 Willie was Meagan's daughter.
Willie was Meagan's parrot.

1 Meagan gave Hannah the hot cookie.

2 Meagan was in the kitchen when Hannah ate the cookie.

3 Willie often said two words together.

Robert and the bear

4 Robert went for a walk with his dog.

5 He was worried when he saw the bears.

6 The mountain lion didn't hurt Robert.

7 The bear and the lion fought for a long time.

3 CRITICAL THINKING **Read the stories again and answer the questions.**

1 How did the animals in the stories help the humans?

2 Which animal do you think was very smart? Why?

Robert and the bear

Robert Biggs lived in Paradise, California. He often went walking near the Sequoia National Forest. One day, he went to the Whiskey Flat Trail, a beautiful walk. Robert was alone, but he enjoyed the quiet. He loved seeing animals and birds on his walks. This time, he saw a family of black bears (a mother and two young cubs) drinking at a river. Robert knew the bears because he sometimes saw them on his walks. Bears in California don't usually attack humans. Robert wasn't worried. He watched the bears playing. Then, suddenly, a mountain lion jumped on his back and bit his arm. Before Robert could fight the lion, the mother bear ran over and attacked it. An adult bear is very big and strong, and after 15 seconds, the mountain lion ran away. The bear looked Robert in the eye and walked back to her cubs. She saved Robert's life.

DEVELOPING Writing

A blog entry about my favorite animal

1 INPUT **Read the text. Why did Rita choose to write about pandas?**

My favorite animal is the giant panda. Pandas live in mountain forests in south central China. They eat bamboo and drink water from rivers. They are my favorite animals because they look so cool. They have thick black and white fur. Giant pandas are very big, but they aren't usually aggressive. That means they don't usually attack people or other animals. They are also very lazy!

In the 1960s, the Chinese government opened some panda reserves – places where pandas and the bamboo they eat are safe – because wild pandas were in danger. In these reserves, there are doctors and experts to take care of baby pandas. Because of this work, there are now nearly 1,860 wild pandas in China. The WWF organization (the World Wide Fund for Nature) has the panda as its symbol, because everyone thinks pandas are cute!

2 ANALYZE **Put the headings in the order you find this information in the text.**

- ☐ What pandas eat and drink
- ☐ What pandas look like
- ☐ Other interesting information
- 1 Where pandas live
- ☐ Why pandas are Rita's favorite animal

3 **Complete the sentences with *but* or *because*.**

1 Pandas are very big, __________ they aren't aggressive.

2 WWF use a panda symbol __________ everyone all around the world thinks they're cute.

3 Experts help pandas with their babies __________ the pandas have problems.

4 Pandas were in danger, __________ now they aren't.

5 Some pandas get sick, __________ doctors can usually help them.

6 I like pandas __________ they look very happy.

4 PLAN **Decide which animal is your favorite. Then read the questions and make notes about your animal for a blog post.**

- What is your favorite animal?
- Where does it live?
- What does it eat and drink?
- What does it look like?
- Why is it your favorite animal?
- What other interesting information can you think of about it?

WRITING TIP: Using a model text

Before you write your own text, read the model text and look for any useful words or phrases you can use.

- *My favorite animal is the …*
- *They are my favorite animals because they …*

5 PRODUCE **Use your notes and the text from Exercise 1 and write a blog post about your favorite animal. Write about 80 words.**

LISTENING

1 11.02 **Listen to Holly talking about volunteering at an animal rescue center. Check (✓) the animals that she talks about.**

2 11.02 **Listen again. Mark the sentences T (true) or F (false).**

0 The boy writes for the school website. *T*
1 Holly volunteers at the Rescue Center after school. ☐
2 She couldn't work at the center when she was 14. ☐
3 They get lots of different pets at the center. ☐
4 Holly liked all the jobs she did at the center. ☐
5 The police found the snake in the police station. ☐
6 Holly loves all animals. ☐
7 Holly wants to work in a zoo when she finishes school. ☐
8 There are some wild animals at the center. ☐

DIALOGUE

3 Complete the conversation with words and phrases from the list.

after that | and | because | ~~but~~ | Poor you | Then

Adriana Did you have a good weekend?
Paulo Yes, it was great, thanks. I went to Miguel's party.
Adriana Oh, right. He invited me, too, [0] *but* I couldn't go.
Paulo Why not?
Adriana My aunt and uncle were here for the weekend, [1] ________ they wanted to take us out.
Paulo That's nice. Where did you go?
Adriana We went to the movies. It was really boring.
Paulo [2] ________ !
Adriana But [3] ________ we went and had pizza. That was good! [4] ________ I ordered an enormous ice cream. I couldn't eat it all, I was so full.
Paulo That's like me at the party. I couldn't dance [5] ________ I was really tired from soccer on Saturday!

4 Read the conversation again and answer the questions.

1 Why couldn't Adriana go to the party?
____
2 Why couldn't Adriana eat all the ice cream?
____
3 Why couldn't Paulo dance at the party?
____

PHRASES FOR FLUENCY

→ SB p.108

5 Put the letters in order to make expressions.

0 dunylsed ... *suddenly ...*
1 lal thrig. ________
2 opor oyu! ________
3 thwa phedapen? ________

6 Complete the conversation with the expressions in Exercise 1.

Eva Do you know what happened to me last weekend?
Katya No, of course not. I wasn't with you last weekend. [0] *What happened?*
Eva [1] ________ , I'll tell you. On Saturday, I was in the café on Main Street, and [2] ________ someone waved at me!
Katya So? Who was it?
Eva It was Jenny Hall.
Katya Jenny Hall? Are you sure? Jenny's in the UK! She moved last year.
Eva Well, she's here on vacation. But it was awful.
Katya Why?
Eva I couldn't remember her name! I called her Annie. And she got really angry with me! She shouted at me!
Katya Oh, [3] ________ . I'm sure that was horrible for you!

BACK-IN-TIME TRAVEL

Welcome to the wonderful world of Back-in-Time Travel.

Talk to William Shakespeare!

As you know, last year the famous Professor Reddy of Bangalore University invented the **Back-in-Time Travel Machine**.

Now, you can go into the past! (Sorry, no future travel yet – maybe next year?)

Sit in the Back-in-Time, choose your time in the past – and whoosh! Off you go!

We are offering one-day trips to the past for only $1,000,000 USD! That's right! Only a million dollars for 24 hours in a past time period that you choose.

But here's some really good news – we have a competition, and the five winners will get a free one-day trip in the Back-in-Time!

All you have to do is write to say what time in the past you want to travel to and why. Write between 10 and 20 words, beginning with "I want to go to …" Here are two examples to help you:

See the dinosaurs!

"I want to go to prehistoric times and see the dinosaurs because they're fantastic animals!" (Frieda, Germany)

"I want to go to 2006 because that's when my country won the World Cup, but I wasn't alive then!" (Bruno, Italy)

But remember – if you win, you must go to the time you wrote about!

Send your ideas to us at: Back-in-Time Travel, P.O. Box 2020, London

Watch the Egyptians building the pyramids!

1 **Read the advertisement. Mark the sentences T (true) or F (false).**

1 A man in New York invented the travel machine. ☐
2 You can travel to the past and into the future. ☐
3 You can buy a trip into the past for one million US dollars. ☐
4 The time trips are for one day. ☐
5 Five people can win a prize in the competition. ☐
6 If you win, you can go to any time in the past you want. ☐

2 **Imagine there's a time machine. Where would you like to go? Write an entry for the competition.**

- Say what time in the past you want to travel to and why.
- Write a paragraph, beginning with "I want to go to …"

12 MOVING AROUND

Grammar rap!

GRAMMAR

Comparative adjectives

→ SB p.112

1 ★☆☆ Underline the comparative adjective in each sentence.

0 The train is <u>faster</u> than the car.
1 His bicycle is more expensive than my bicycle.
2 Surfing is more dangerous than tennis.
3 The weather in the winter is worse than in the summer.
4 Spanish is easier than Chinese.
5 Your phone is better than my phone.
6 My house is further from school than your house.
7 Their car is bigger than our car.
8 Salad is healthier than fries.

2 ★☆☆ Complete the table with the correct adjective forms.

adjective	comparative
0 dirty	*dirtier*
1 beautiful	
2 cold	
3	curlier
4 hot	
5	cleaner
6	shorter
7 ugly	
8	more boring
9 sad	
10 warm	
11 lovely	
12	slower
13	more interesting

3 ★★☆ Look at the table and mark the sentences T (true) or F (false). Correct the false sentences.

	Leaves Boston	Arrives Washington, D.C.	Price
train	8 a.m.	1 p.m.	$140
bus	5 a.m.	5 p.m.	$35
plane	10 a.m.	11:30 a.m.	$75

0 The train is cheaper than the bus. [*F*]
The train is more expensive than the bus.
1 The bus arrives later than the train. [ ]
______
2 The bus is slower than the plane. [ ]
______
3 The bus is more expensive than the plane. [ ]
______
4 The plane is faster than the train. [ ]
______
5 The plane arrives earlier than the bus. [ ]
______

4 ★★★ Use the table in Exercise 3 to write sentences. Use comparative adjectives.

0 bus / early / train
The bus leaves earlier than the train.
1 train / fast / bus
______
2 plane / expensive / bus
______
3 train / slow / plane
______
4 bus / late / plane
______
5 bus / cheap / train
______

PRONUNCIATION
Word stress – comparatives
Go to page 121.

5 ★★★ Look at the pictures and write sentences to compare the two taxi companies. Use the adjectives in the list to help you.

big | ~~clean~~ | dangerous | dirty
expensive | fast | good | safe

0 *Lidia's limos are cleaner than Tim's taxis.*
1 ______
2 ______
3 ______
4 ______
5 ______
6 ______
7 ______

6 ★★★ Complete the sentences so they are true for you.

1 I'm ______ than my parents.
2 My best friend is ______ than me.
3 English classes are ______ than math classes.
4 Parrots are ______ than cats.
5 Summer is ______ than winter.
6 Walking is ______ than cycling.

one / ones

→ SB p.115

7 ★☆☆ Circle the correct options.

0 Can I have a look at those jeans? The *one* / *(ones)* in the window.
1 Don't buy me a coffee. I don't want *one* / *ones*.
2 I like most movies, but I don't like *one* / *ones* about war.
3 I can't give you a piece of paper because I don't have *one* / *ones*.
4 I have some apples. Would you like *one* / *ones*?
5 I'm interested in cars, and I really like Italian *one* / *ones*.

8 ★★☆ Write *one* into the dialogues in the correct place.

0 A Where's your house?
B My house is the first *one* on the left.

1 A How was your birthday?
B Great. I got a lot of presents, but my favorite was a book from my dad.

2 A Which dress did you buy?
B Well, I love red, so I bought the red.

3 A How is your new computer?
B It's faster than my old, and it's easier to use.

4 A Is that your cousin over there?
B Yes, he's the with the glasses.

GET IT RIGHT!

one and *ones*

We use *one* or *ones* after an adjective when we want to avoid repeating a noun.

✓ *I like this song; it's a good one.*
✗ *I like this song; ~~it's a good song.~~*
✓ *I wore my new shoes – the red ones.*
✗ *I wore my new shoes – ~~the red shoes.~~*

Replace one of the nouns with *one* or *ones*.

0 How much are the cakes? I mean the big cakes.
How much are the cakes? I mean the big ones.
1 These tickets are expensive. We can find cheaper tickets.
______
2 This pen isn't good. I have a better pen in my bag.
______
3 The blue jeans are too big. The black jeans are much better.
______
4 All of the buses go there, but the red bus is the fastest.
______
5 Where are my black shoes? They were next to my brown shoes.
______

VOCABULARY

Transportation

→ SB p.112

1 ★☆☆ **Find and circle five more types of transportation in the word snake.**

agemotorcycleasehelicopternmbdplanerkutaxilfqferryipatrainbgh

2 ★★☆ **Put the letters in order to make the column titles. Then complete the table with words from Exercise 1.**

no het ardo 0 *on the road*	no sairl 1 ______	ni eth ria 2 ______	no tware 3 ______
motorcycle			

3 ★★★ **Match the words from Exercise 1 with their definitions.**

0 It flies in the air, but it doesn't have wings. *helicopter*
1 It travels on rails and is very long. ______
2 It flies in the air. It has wings. ______
3 It travels on water and carries a lot of people. ______
4 You pay someone to drive you. ______
5 It drives on the road but only has two wheels. ______

Geographical places

→ SB p.115

4 ★★☆ **Find the places in the word search. Write the words under the pictures.**

Q	H	C	A	E	B	W	W	M
H	E	E	O	F	G	S	O	S
F	V	S	U	D	R	U	R	E
O	M	C	D	U	N	A	K	R
R	H	R	R	T	B	A	E	U
E	T	P	A	B	L	V	S	C
S	X	I	E	F	I	P	B	T
T	N	C	K	R	R	T	D	B
Z	D	L	E	I	F	C	O	V

0

forest

1

______

2

______

3

______

4

______

5

______

6

______

7

______

5 ★★☆ **Match the geographical places with the famous examples.**

1 mountain ☐
2 lake ☐
3 river ☐
4 beach ☐
5 ocean ☐

a The Nile, The Amazon, The Yangtze
b Aconcagua, K2, Kilimanjaro
c Copacabana, Bondi, Kuta
d Atlantic, Pacific, Indian
e Michigan, Titicaca, Victoria

6 ★★★ **Complete the sentences with examples from your own country.**

1 My favorite beach is ______ .
2 The highest mountain is ______ .
3 A famous lake is ______ .
4 The longest river is ______ .
5 ______ is a good place to go on vacation.
6 ______ is a beautiful place in the winter.

REFERENCE

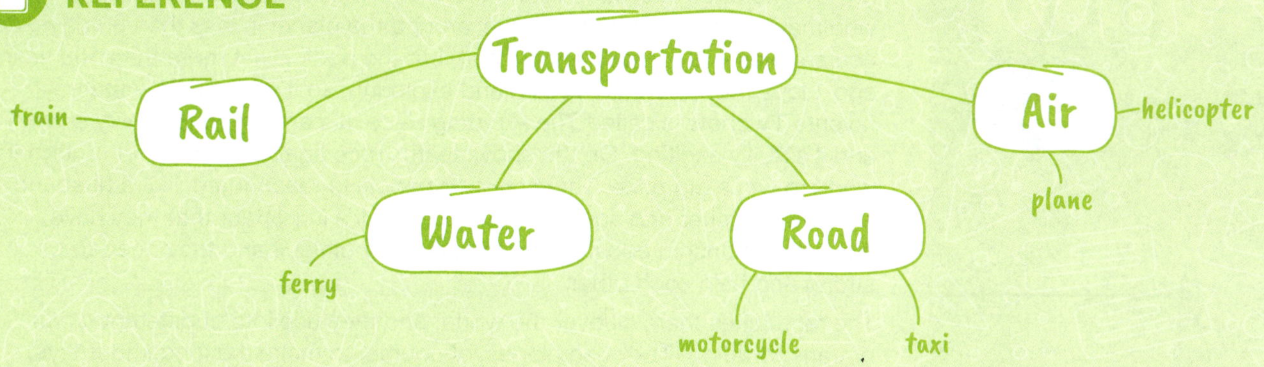

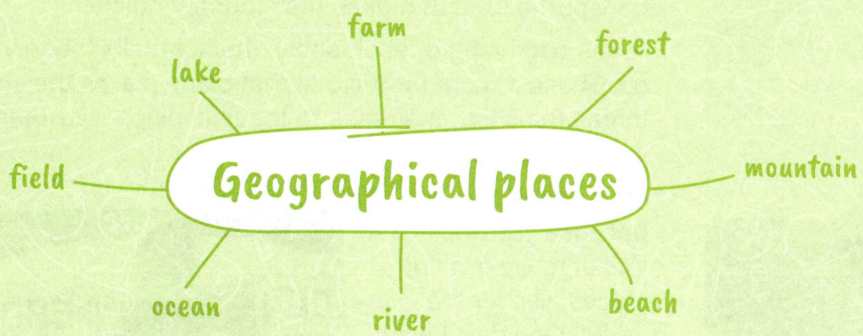

VOCABULARY *EXTRA*

1 Label the pictures of day and night with the words from the list.

cloud | moon | sky | star | sun

2 Choose the correct answers (A, B, or C).

1 The color of the sky is really __________ .
A blue B red C no color

2 The sun is __________ million kilometers from our planet.
A 98.7 B 149.6 C 203.5

3 A cloud is __________ .
A air with water or ice in it B hot C water or ice

4 The Moon goes around the Earth every __________ .
A 30.25 days B 29.98 days C 27.32 days

5 There are about __________ stars in the universe.
A 1 billion B 1 trillion C 1 billion trillion

Answers: 1 A – We see blue light because of air molecules; 2 B; 3 A; 4 C; 5 C (very approximately)

RACING AROUND THE WORLD!

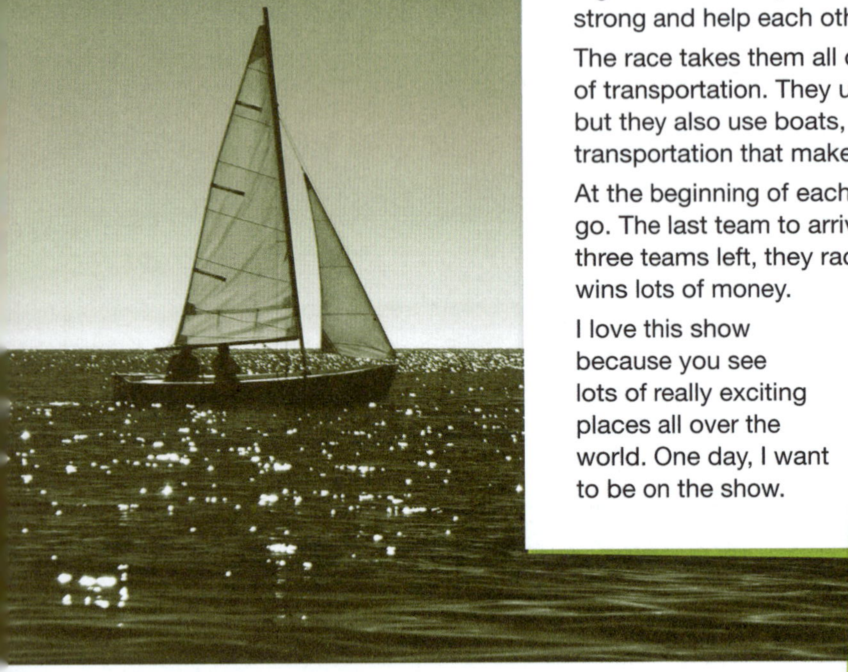

My favorite book is called *Around the World in 80 Days*. It's the story of a man who makes a bet that he can travel around the planet in less than 80 days. Of course, these days that's not difficult, but the book is set more than 100 years ago. I love the idea of adventure and exploring, so it's no surprise that my favorite TV show is called *The Amazing Race*. It's an American reality show, and it's really exciting. On the show, teams race against each other around the world to win a big prize. There are two people on each team, like a husband and wife, a father and son, best friends, etc. It's important that they have a good relationship because the race is really difficult and they need to be strong and help each other.

The race takes them all over the world, and they use lots of different types of transportation. They use planes, of course, to make the longer journeys, but they also use boats, taxis, buses, helicopters, bikes, cars, trains – any transportation that makes their journey quicker.

At the beginning of each show, the host tells the teams where they have to go. The last team to arrive at that place leaves the show. When there are only three teams left, they race to the final place. The team that arrives first usually wins lots of money.

I love this show because you see lots of really exciting places all over the world. One day, I want to be on the show.

READING

1 Read the blog. Which of these types of transportation is not mentioned?

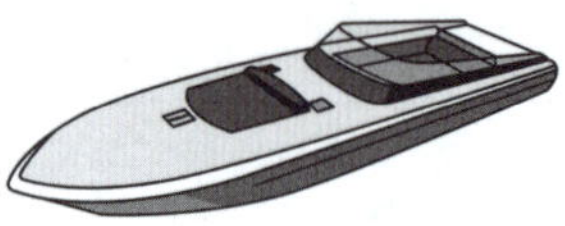 ☐

 ☐

 ☐

 ☐

☐

 ☐

2 Read the blog again and match the sentence halves.

0 *Around the World in 80 Days* [g]
1 *The Amazing Race* ☐
2 The race is ☐
3 The people on the teams ☐
4 The teams race ☐
5 The teams use ☐
6 The last team to arrive ☐
7 In the final ☐
8 The winning team ☐

a between teams of two people.
b all over the world.
c leaves the show.
d gets a lot of money.
e is a TV show from the US.
f a lot of different types of transportation.
g is a famous book.
h know each other.
i there are three teams.

3 CRITICAL THINKING **Do you want to be on *The Amazing Race*? Why or why not? Write a short paragraph (60–80 words).**

DEVELOPING *Writing*

Writing about a trip

1 INPUT **Read about Eric and Alexia's favorite trips. Do they prefer leaving or coming home?**

____

Eric

My favorite trip is the one I make every Saturday morning to play basketball. I leave my house at about nine o'clock and get on my bike to bike the three kilometers to the sports club. It takes me about 15 minutes. At the club, I meet my team, and we play a game. Then I get on my bike and ride back home. I like the trip there because I get excited about playing basketball. I don't like the trip back so much because I'm usually very tired. But when I have a good game, the trip back is great, too, because I think about the game.

Alexia

The trip I like best is the one from my house to my dad's house. My dad lives in Texas, and three times every year, I fly there to spend some time with him. The trip starts really early. The taxi picks me up from my house at 4 a.m.! But that's OK, because I'm always really happy. It's only 30 minutes to the airport, but I can't wait to get there. The plane trip is about four hours. It's not very exciting, but I usually listen to music or go to sleep. My dad always meets me at the airport, and then he drives me to his house. We don't stop talking the whole trip. I never like the trip back. I'm always really sad to leave.

2 ANALYZE **Read the texts again and complete the table.**

	from	to	transportation	time it takes	why I like it
Eric					
Alexia					

3 PLAN **Think about your favorite trip and make notes to complete the table so it is true for you.**

	from	to	transportation	time	why I like it
Me					

4 PRODUCE **Use your notes to write a text about your favorite trip. Write 35–50 words.**

WRITING TIP: Useful language

- *My favorite trip is the one I make* (every Saturday morning) *to* (play basketball).
- *The trip I like best is the one from* (my house) *to* (my dad's house).
- *The trip starts* (really early).
- *It takes me about* (15 minutes).
- *I like the trip there because* (I get excited about playing basketball.)
- *I don't like the trip back* (so much) *because* (I'm usually very tired).

LISTENING

1 12.02 **Listen to the conversation. Where is Jill? Who is she talking to?**

____

2 12.02 **Listen again and circle the correct answers (A, B, or C).**

0 Where does Jill want to go?
- A Washington, D.C.
- (B) New York
- C Boston

1 What time is the next train?
- A 
- B 
- C 

2 How often is there a train?
- A every 15 minutes
- B every 30 minutes
- C every 50 minutes

3 How long is the trip?
- A 40 minutes
- B 35 minutes
- C 45 minutes

4 When is Jill returning?
- A today
- B tomorrow
- C on the weekend

5 How much is the ticket?
- A $7.80
- B $8.70
- C $17.80

6 What platform is the train leaving from?
- A 3
- B 4
- C 5

7 What time does Jill get the train?
- A 
- B 
- C 

DIALOGUE

3 **Circle the correct options. Then put the conversation in order.**

☐	**Assistant**	The trip is [1]*a quarter / half* of an hour.
☐	**Assistant**	OK, that's $7.80, please.
☐	**Assistant**	Platform 5. Have a [2]*good / boring* trip.
☐	**Assistant**	Let me see. There's a train every 15 minutes, so the next one is at three thirty.
☐	**Assistant**	Do you want one-way ticket or a round-trip ticket?
1	**Assistant**	Good afternoon. [3]*How / Who* can I help you?
☐	**Woman**	That's great. And how long does it take?
☐	**Woman**	Thank you.
☐	**Woman**	I want to [4]*go / come* to New York. What time's the next train?
☐	**Woman**	Just one more thing. What platform does the train leave [5]*from / at*?
☐	**Woman**	30 minutes. That's fast. Can I have a ticket, please?
☐	**Woman**	A round-trip ticket, please. I'm coming back later.

Train to THINK

Comparing

4 **Complete the diagram with the words from the list. Then use your own ideas and write six more words.**

boring | dangerous | exciting | expensive | fun | relaxing

5 **Write sentences to compare the two different**

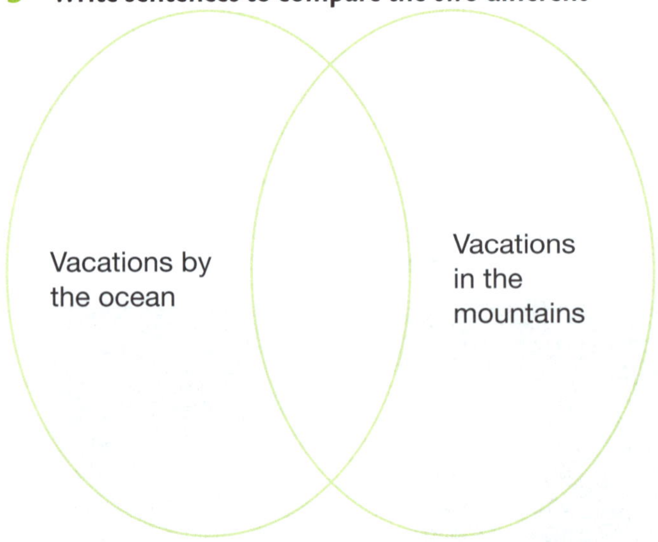

types of vacations in Exercise 4.

____

____

____

TOWARDS A2 Key for Schools

EXAM SKILLS: READING

Answering open cloze questions

1 Read Matteo's answers in the task below. How many did he get right? How many did he get wrong?

Complete the text about travelling to and from school. Write ONE word for each space.

I live [0] ___*in*___ a small town and my school is about six kilometres away. Most days I take the school bus. It stops outside my house [1] ___*at*___ 7.30 every morning. In the summer, when the weather [2] ___*are*___ good, I usually cycle to school. It's quicker [3] ___*than*___ the bus because the bus stops all the time. The problem with the bike is when my school bag is too heavy. Then it's [4] ___*not*___ fun.
Sometimes I wake up late and [5] ___*mis*___ the school bus. Mum takes me to school [6] ___*in*___ the car. She doesn't like this [7] ___*because*___ she needs to get to work, too. Once I missed the bus home and I had to [8] ___*tired*___ home. It took me more than [9] ___*half an*___ hour to walk. I don't want [10] ___*to*___ do that again.

READING TIP:

- Read the instructions carefully. Underline the key words. Words like *circle, tick, choose* and *underline* tell you how to complete the question. Look for other important information, for example, *Write ONE word for each space.*
- When you have finished, read your answers again. Have you followed the instructions? Have you used the correct type of word (verb, noun, adjective, etc.)? Have you used the singular and plural forms correctly? Is your spelling correct?
- Don't leave any gaps. If you don't know the answer, guess!

2 Put Matteo's mistakes under the correct heading. Write the number.

Used more than one word	Used the wrong type of word (adjective instead of verb)	Used singular and plural forms incorrectly	Used incorrect spelling
9			

3 Correct Matteo's mistakes. Write the correct words next to the numbers in Exercise 2.

4 Complete the text about favourite holidays. Write ONE word for each space.

My favourite holidays [0] ___*are*___ beach holidays. I like the sun [1] ________ the sea. I usually go on beach holidays [2] ________ the summer with my family. Sometimes Dad drives and sometimes we [3] ________ the train. Last year, we went [4] ________ holiday in the countryside. We stayed on [5] ________ farm. There was a river and a lake and lots [6] ________ fields, too. It was OK, but I prefer beach holidays. The weather by the sea is usually hotter [7] ________ in the countryside. Dad wants to [8] ________ on holiday in the mountains this year. I'm [9] ________ happy about that idea. I don't want another year away [10] ________ the beach.

CONSOLIDATION

LISTENING

1 🔊 12.03 **Listen to Caleb and circle the correct answers (A, B, or C).**

1 How old is Caleb's brother?
A eight B nine C ten

2 At the zoo, which animals scared Caleb's brother?
A the elephants B the lions C the tigers

3 How many jaguars were there?
A two B three C four

2 🔊 12.03 **Listen again and answer the questions.**

1 Why did Caleb's family go to the zoo?
____

2 Who took photos at the zoo?
____

3 What was Caleb happy about?
____

4 What did Caleb think about the visit to the zoo?
____

5 Why was Caleb sorry for the jaguars?
____

6 What two things does Caleb think zoo animals need?
____

GRAMMAR

3 Complete the sentences with the correct form of the words in parentheses.

1 Yesterday, I ________ some money on the street. (find)

2 For my last birthday, my parents ________ me tickets for a concert. (give)

3 My friends and I ________ to the movies three times last month. (go)

4 I arrived home late last night, but I ________ any noise. (not make)

5 Yesterday's test was ________ than the one on Friday. (difficult)

6 ________ you ________ that movie on TV last Sunday night? (see)

7 The weather today is ________ than yesterday. (bad)

8 I practice a lot, and I'm getting ________ every day! (good)

9 I ________ many presents for my birthday. (not get)

10 Are tigers ________ than jaguars? (big)

VOCABULARY

4 Circle the odd one out in each list. Explain your reasons.

0 safe clean (homework)
It's a noun – the other two are adjectives.

1 motorcycle plane helicopter
____

2 shopping homework a mistake
____

3 forest ocean lake
____

4 train river subway
____

5 a break a good time photos
____

6 boat ferry taxi
____

7 a mistake a shower a noise
____

8 breakfast elephant horse
____

9 field beach farm
____

5 Use a word or phrase from Exercise 4 to complete each sentence.

1 Shh! Don't make ________ or that pretty bird will fly away.

2 We went for a walk in the ________ this morning. The trees were very beautiful.

3 My mom doesn't like me riding my bike in the city. She thinks it isn't ________.

4 This party's great. I'm having ________.

5 Her name's Julie, but I made ________ and called her Jenny.

6 I like taking ________ after soccer to get clean again!

7 We went to the beach, but I didn't swim in the ________ – I think it's dangerous.

8 I'm really tired. Let's take ________ and have some coffee.

DIALOGUE

6 12.04 **Complete the dialogue with the words and phrases from the list. There are two extra words/phrases. Then listen and check.**

All right | better | came | cheaper | could | didn't | Did | lovely | made | That's terrible | suddenly | What happened

Jin How was your weekend at the beach?

Maria Oh, awful. Everything went wrong.

Jin Oh, no. [1]________________ ?

Maria Well, first, we missed the bus.

Jin But you got there in the end?

Maria Oh, yes, we got there. We always stay at the same hotel. But it's very expensive, so this year Dad said, "Let's stay at a [2]________________ hotel." I said, "Dad! If our usual hotel is more expensive, that's because it's [3]________________ than the cheaper ones." [4]________________ he listen? No, he didn't. The hotel was horrible! I [5]________________ sleep at all – there were cars outside all night. They [6]________________ a lot of noise!

Jin [7]________________ , but what about the beach?

Maria The beach there is really [8]________________ . We like it a lot. So we went there on the first day – but [9]________________ it started to rain! We [10]________________ home a day early. The weekend was … well, it was horrible.

READING

The Scottish Highlands – there's nowhere more beautiful!

Are you thinking about taking a break? Then try the Scottish Highlands. This lovely part of Scotland has forests, rivers, lakes – called *lochs* in Scotland – and, of course, mountains! The mountains are beautiful and quiet, with fantastic walks. Check the weather first, though, as it can change very quickly!

The town of Inverness is the capital of the Highlands. It has lots of interesting stores and restaurants. Try haggis, a Scottish speciality. You can also visit Cawdor Castle, 14 miles away. Inverness is on the coast, so there's a beach, but it can be cold, even in the summer!

Another place to see is Loch Ness, the lake famous for its monster, Nessie! Visit the museum or take a boat trip across the loch.

There are a lot of hotels and bed-and-breakfast places in the Highlands. The B&Bs are cheaper, but sometimes they're as good as hotels. The breakfasts are really big, so expect to be full all day! They often serve afternoon tea, with sandwiches and cake, too.

You can get to Inverness or Fort William by train, but to visit the lochs and the mountains, it's easier to drive.

Why not visit the Highlands soon? We'd love to see you!

7 **Read the web page. Mark the sentences T (true) or F (false).**

1 Lakes in Scotland have a different name. ☐
2 You have to check the weather before you go for a walk. ☐
3 There isn't a lot to do in Inverness. ☐
4 Loch Ness has a famous monster. ☐
5 B&Bs are more expensive than hotels. ☐
6 At the B&B places, you usually get a small breakfast. ☐
7 You can't visit everywhere in the Highlands by train. A car is better. ☐

WRITING

8 **Write a paragraph about a nice area that you know. Write 60–80 words. Use the questions to help you.**

- What is it called?
- What are the good things about it?
- What can people do there?
- How can you get there?

PRONUNCIATION

UNIT 7

Vowel sound /ɔr/

1 7.01 **Listen to these words. They all contain the /ɔr/ sound. Underline the sound in each word.**

0 orange
1 morning
2 tour
3 door
4 forty
5 important
6 quarter
7 short
8 snowboarding
9 sport
10 store
11 floor

2 Complete the sentences with the words in Exercise 1.

0 Please close the *door* when you go out.
1 This city is beautiful. Let's go on a ____________ .
2 Please buy some food at the ____________ .
3 English is a very ____________ language.
4 The office is on the fourth ____________ .
5 I have art class in the ____________ .
6 Jenny likes ____________ in the mountains in the winter.
7 My favorite ____________ is volleyball.
8 I'm thirsty. Can I have a glass of ____________ juice, please?
9 My hair is long, but my friend's is ____________ .
10 My first class at school starts at a ____________ to nine.
11 It's my father's birthday today. He's ____________ years old.

3 7.02 **Listen, check, and repeat.**

UNIT 8

Intonation – listing items

1 Complete the lists. Then draw a ↗ and a ↘ to show where intonation rises and falls in each list.

arm | Brazil | catch | coat | headphones | ~~June~~ | library | Russian | rugby | stove | spring | wife

0 March ↗, April ↗, May ↗, and *June* ↘
1 son, daughter, husband, and ____________
2 Japanese, British, ____________ , and Turkish
3 ____________ , skirt, socks, and shoes
4 snowboarding, gymnastics, golf, and ____________
5 summer, ____________ , winter, and fall
6 watch, choose, throw, and ____________
7 ____________ , shower, fridge, and armchair
8 Australia, Scotland, ____________ , and Japan
9 body, ____________ , leg, and face
10 tablet, GPS, ____________ , and laptop
11 ____________ , restaurant, museum, and bank

2 8.01 **Listen, check, and repeat.**

UNIT 9
Intonation – giving two choices

1 9.01 **Complete the dialogue with the words in the list. Then listen and check.**

chicken | fish | fries | ice cream
pineapple | ~~soup~~ | tea | water

↗ ↘

Waiter Would you like salad or [0] *soup* ?
Woman Salad, please.

☐ ☐

Waiter Chicken or [1] ______________ ?
Woman I think I'll have [2] ______________ today – with [3] ______________ , please.
Waiter Would you like dessert?
Woman Yes, please.

☐ ☐

Waiter Cake or [4] ______________ ?
Woman I'd prefer fruit – some [5] ______________ , please.
Waiter Would you like something to drink?
Woman Yes, please – just some [6] ______________ . And a cup of [7] ______________ after the meal. Thank you.

2 9.01 **Draw ↗ or ↘ above the waiter's questions. Then listen, check, and repeat.**

UNIT 10
Simple past regular verbs

1 **Say the verbs in the list in the past tense and decide if they are one syllable or two. Then write the verbs in the correct column.**

~~dance~~ | ~~hate~~ | help | like | live | need
play | start | wait | walk | want | work

one syllable	two syllables
danced	*hated*

2 10.01 **Listen, check, and repeat.**

3 **Complete the rule.**

We only say /ɪd/ when the final sound in the word is a / ______________ / or a / ______________ /.

UNIT 11
Short vowel sound /ʊ/

1 **Circle the odd sound out.**

0	(cook)	true	food
1	house	shout	could
2	June	put	who
3	room	you	woods
4	pull	fun	son
5	foot	put	jump
6	move	zoo	good
7	funny	woolly	sunny
8	two	room	book
9	push	run	bus
10	cousin	couldn't	country

2 11.01 **Listen, check, and repeat.**

UNIT 12
Word stress – comparatives

1 **Write the comparative form of the adjectives. Underline the stressed syllable.**

0	slow	*slower*	8	big	________
1	small	________	9	hot	________
2	quick	________	10	funny	________
3	cheap	________	11	easy	________
4	fast	________	12	healthy	________
5	cold	________	13	happy	________
6	safe	________	14	far	________
7	close	________	15	good	________

2 12.01 **Listen, check, and repeat.**

3 **Complete the rule.**

When adding *-er* to make a comparative, the *first* / *second* syllable is always stressed.

GRAMMAR REFERENCE

UNIT 7

can (ability)

1 **We use *can* / *can't* to talk about ability.**

*I **can** swim.*
*I **can't** drive a car.*
*He **can** play the guitar.*
*He **can't** sing.*

2 **The form is *can* / *can't* + the base form of the verb. To make questions, we use *Can* + subject + the base form of the verb. (We don't use *do* / *does* with *can* in questions or negative forms.)**

*It's very small – I **can't read** it. (NOT: ~~I don't can read~~ it.)*
***Can you play** this game? (NOT: ~~Do you can play~~ this game?)*

3 **Short answers are *Yes, … can* or *No, … can't*.**

*Can he swim? **Yes, he can.***
*Can you sing? **No, I can't.***

Prepositions of time

We use different prepositions to talk about time.

1 **With times of the day, we use *at*.**

*School starts **at** 8 o'clock.*
*The train leaves **at** seven thirty.*

2 **With months and seasons, we use *in*.**

*It always rains **in** December.*
*We play soccer **in** the winter.*

3 **With days of the week, we use *on*.**

*I go to the movies **on** Saturday.*
*There's a test at school **on** Monday.*

UNIT 8

Present continuous

1 **We use the present continuous to talk about things that are happening at the moment of speaking.**

*Please be quiet – **I'm watching** a movie.*
*They're in the dining room – they**'re having** dinner.*
*Dad's in his office, but he **isn't working**.*
*Hey, Alex – **are** you **listening** to me?*

2 **We form the present continuous with the simple present of *be* + the *-ing* form of the main verb. Questions and negatives are formed with the question/negative form of *be* + the *-ing* form of the main verb.**

*I**'m watching** a movie, but I**'m not enjoying** it.*
*They**'re playing** soccer, but they **aren't playing** well.*
***Are** you **having** a good time? Yes, we **are**.*
***Is** she **doing** her homework? No, she **isn't**.*

3 **If the verb ends in *-e*, we omit the *e* before adding *-ing*. If the verb ends in a consonant + vowel + consonant, we double the consonant before adding *-ing*.**

leave	*We're **leaving** now.*
get	*It's **getting** dark – let's go home.*

like / don't like + -ing

When we use the verbs *(don't) like, love, hate,* and another verb, we usually use the *-ing* form of the other verb.

*We **love living** here.*
*I **like dancing** at parties.*
*She **doesn't like listening** to classical music.*
*They **hate going** to the movies.*

UNIT 9

must / mustn't

We use *must / mustn't* to talk about rules.

1 **We use *must* to say that it's necessary to do something.**

*We **must leave** now.*

*You **must go** to the doctor.*

2 **We use *mustn't* to say that it's necessary not to do something.**

*You **mustn't tell** other people.*

*We **mustn't be** late.*

3 **The form is *must / mustn't* + the base form of the verb. We don't use *do / does* in negative sentences.**

*You must **ask** me first.*

*I mustn't **eat** a lot of snacks before dinner.*

(NOT: ~~*I don't must eat a lot of snacks before dinner.*~~)

can (asking for permission)

1 **We often use *Can I* + verb to ask for permission (ask if it's OK) to do something.**

***Can I ask** a question, please?*

***Can I watch** the game on TV now?*

2 **We use *can* or *can't* to give or refuse permission.**

***Can I use** your phone?* *Yes, you **can**.*

*No, sorry, you **can't**. I'm using it.*

I'd like … / Would you like …?

1 **We use *would* (*'d*) + *like* to ask for something, or to offer something, in a nice way. It is more polite than *want*.**

***I'd like** a sandwich, please.*

***Would you like** a dessert?*

2 ***I'd like* is the short form of *I would like*. We almost always use it in speaking and informal writing.**

UNIT 10

Simple past: *was / wasn't; were / weren't; there was / were*

1 **We use the simple past form of *to be* to talk about actions and events in the past.**

*It **was** a lovely day yesterday.*

*They **were** at school last Friday.*

2 **We form the simple past of *be* like this:**

singular	plural
I **was**	we **were**
you **were**	you **were**
he/she/it **was**	they **were**

3 **We form the negative by adding *not* (*was not, were not*). In speaking and informal writing, we almost always use the short forms *wasn't* and *weren't*.**

*I **wasn't** at home last night.*

*She **wasn't** at the party.*

*You **weren't** very happy yesterday.*

*They **weren't** with us at the concert.*

4 **The simple past of *there is(n't) / there are(n't)* is *there was(n't) / there were(n't)*.**

***There was** a lot of rain yesterday.*

***There weren't** any interesting shows on TV last night.*

Simple past: *Was he …? / Were you …?*

We form questions by putting the verb before the subject.

***Were** you late on Monday morning?*

***Was** she at the movies with you?*

Simple past: regular verbs

1 **We use the simple past to talk about actions and events in the past.**

*I **played** video games yesterday.*

*They **liked** the movie on Friday.*

2 **With regular verbs, we form the simple past by adding *-ed*. It is the same for all subjects.**

*He **closed** the window.*

*The movie **finished** after midnight.*

*You **called** me three times last night.*

*We **wanted** to see them.*

3 **When the verb ends in *-e*, we only add *-d*. When the verb ends in consonant + *-y*, we change the *y* to *i* and then we add *-ed*.**

*We **loved** the concert on Sunday.*

*They **studied** for a long time before the test.*

UNIT 11

Simple past: irregular verbs

1 Many English verbs are irregular. This means that the simple past forms are different – they don't have the usual *-ed* ending. For example:

*go – **went***
*make – **made***
*give – **gave***
*take – **took***
*put – **put***

2 For every irregular verb, you need to remember the simple past form. There is a list of irregular verbs on page 128.

Simple past (negative)

We form negatives in the simple past with *didn't (did not)* and the base form of the verb. It's the same for both regular and irregular verbs. It's the same for all subjects.

talk	*I **didn't talk**.*
like	*You **didn't like** it.*
give	*She **didn't give** me a present.*
go	*He **didn't go** to town.*
take	*We **didn't take** any photos.*
make	*They **didn't make** any money.*

Simple past (questions)

We form questions in the simple past with *Did* + subject + the base form of the verb. It's the same for all verbs (regular and irregular) and for all subjects.

see	***Did** I **see** you in town on Saturday?*
do	***Did** you **do** the homework last night?*
go	***Did** your brother **go** to the same school?*
take	***Did** they **take** you to the movies?*

could / couldn't (ability)

To talk about ability in the past, we use *could/ couldn't* + the base form of a verb.

*When I was small, I **could walk** on my hands.*
*We went to New York, but we **couldn't go** to the Statue of Liberty because it was closed.*

UNIT 12

Comparative adjectives

1 We use the comparative form of the adjective + *than* to compare two things.

*My sister is **younger than** me.*
*Australia is **smaller than** Brazil.*
*My new smartphone is **better than** the old one.*

2 With short adjectives, we normally add *-er*.

*new – new**er***
*quiet – quiet**er***

With adjectives that end in *-e*, we just add *-r*.

*nice – nice**r***
*fine – fine**r***

With adjectives of two syllables that end with consonant + *-y*, we change the *y* to *i* and add *-er*.

*easy – eas**ier***
*healthy – health**ier***

With adjectives that end in consonant + vowel + consonant, we double the final consonant and add *-er*.

*big – big**ger***
*hot – hot**ter***

3 With longer adjectives (i.e., with two or more syllables), we don't change the adjective – we put *more* in front of it.

*expensive – **more expensive***
*dangerous – **more dangerous***

4 Some adjectives are irregular – this means they have a different comparative form.

*good – **better***
*bad – **worse***
*far – **further***

one / ones

1 Sometimes we don't want to repeat a noun. We can use *one* or *ones* in order not to repeat it.

*The pizza was delicious – I want another (~~pizza~~) **one**.*
*These shoes are very expensive – I want cheaper (~~shoes~~) **ones**.*

2 We use *one* to replace a singular noun and *ones* to replace a plural noun.

*This red shirt is OK, but the blue **one** is nicer.*
(one replaces shirt)
*I don't want to play these old games – let's buy some new **ones**. (ones replaces games)*

IRREGULAR VERBS

Base form	Simple past
be	was/were
begin	began
buy	bought
can	could
catch	caught
choose	chose
come	came
do	did
draw	drew
drink	drank
drive	drove
eat	ate
fall	fell
feel	felt
find	found
fly	flew
get	got
give	gave
go	went
have	had
hear	heard
keep	kept
know	knew
learn	learned
leave	left

Base form	Simple past
light	lit
make	made
meet	met
pay	paid
put	put
read /riːd/	read /red/
ride	rode
run	ran
say	said
see	saw
send	sent
sing	sang
sit	sat
sleep	slept
speak	spoke
stand	stood
take	took
teach	taught
tell	told
think	thought
understand	understood
wake	woke
wear	wore
write	wrote

ACKNOWLEDGEMENTS

Author

The authors and publishers acknowledge the following sources of copyright material and are grateful for the permissions granted. While every effort has been made, it has not always been possible to identify the sources of all the material used, or to trace all copyright holders. If any omissions are brought to our notice, we will be happy to include the appropriate acknowledgements on reprinting and in the next update to the digital edition, as applicable.

Key: UW = Unit

Photography

All the photographs are sourced from Getty Images.

U7: gazanfer/iStock/Getty Images Plus; JoyImage/iStock/Getty Images Plus; Bryn Lennon/Getty Images Sport; Junya Nishigawa - PARAPHOTO/Getty Images Sport; Fuse/Corbis; kyoshino/iStock/Getty Images Plus; **U8:** Inti St Clair; joingate/iStock/Getty Images Plus; Kim Grosz/EyeEm; **U9:** Emma Farrer/Moment; Science Photo Library; Floortje/E+; Byjeng/iStock/Getty Images Plus; Yothin Sanchai/EyeEm; Natthakan Jommanee/EyeEm; Nattawut Lakjit/EyeEm; bergamont/iStock/Getty Images Plus; eli_asenova/E+; ManuWe/E+; Creativeye99/E+; FotografiaBasica/iStock/Getty Images Plus; Getty Images/EyeEm; Marat Musabirov/iStock/Getty Images Plus; Hyrma/iStock/Getty Images Plus; Nirut Punshiri/EyeEm; LauriPatterson/E+; pamela_d_mcadams/iStock/Getty Images Plus; Simon Belcher; AnnaPustynnikova/iStock/Getty Images Plus; Nettiya Nithascharukul/EyeEm; Burcu Atalay Tankut/Moment; **U10:** Underwood Archives/Archive Photos; WPA Pool/Getty Images News; IMAGEMORE Co.,Ltd.; Sylvain Lefevre/Getty Images Entertainment; Print Collector/Hulton Archive; George Pachantouris/Moment; Jesse Grant/Getty Images Entertainment; Noam Galai/Getty Images Entertainment; Topical Press Agency/Hulton Archive; INDRANIL MUKHERJEE/AFP; UniversalImagesGroup/Universal Images Group; Universal History Archive/Universal Images Group; SDI Productions/E+; **U11:** izusek/E+; moodboard; MichaelJust/iStock/Getty Images Plus; Chris McNeill/500px Prime; Fernán Quetequitenloviajao/500Px Plus; by Simon Gakhar/Moment Open; CreativeNature_nl/iStock/Getty Images Plus; Mark Hamblin/Oxford Scientific; Andrea Edwards/EyeEm; Philartphace/E+; shuchun ke/500px/500Px Plus; Maria Jeffs/iStock/Getty Images Plus; Sergio Amiti/Moment; kickers/E+; Image Source; DEA PICTURE LIBRARY/De Agostini Picture Library; FierceAbin/E+; Richard Nowitz/DigitalVision; **U12:** Mike Kemp; Luis Franceschi/EyeEm; Steve Raymer/Corbis D;ocumentary; wsfurlan/E+; MicroStockHub/iStock/Getty Images Plus; simonbradfield/E+.

The following photograph is sourced from an other source/library.

U10: Mike Blenkinsop/Alamy Stock Photo.

Cover photography by Konstantin Tronin/Shutterstock; © Marco Bottigelli/Moment/Getty Images

Illustrations

U7: Dusan Lakicevic; Ben Scruton; Adam Linley; Mark Ruffle; **U8**: Emma Nyari; **U9** & **U10**: Adam Linley; **U11**: Mark Ruffle; **U12**: Dusan Lakicevic; Martin Sanders; Adam Linley.

The Vlog & Grammar Rap Video Stills: Silversun Media Group

Audio Production: CityVox, New York